Thomas Jefferson

Other books in The American Statesmen series:

George Washington by Henry Cabot Lodge

Thomas Jefferson

JOHN T. MORSE JR.

The AMERICAN STATESMEN *Series*

Foreword by George Grant

CUMBERLAND HOUSE
NASHVILLE, TENNESSEE

Published by
CUMBERLAND HOUSE PUBLISHING, INC.
431 Harding Industrial Drive
Nashville, TN 37211

Foreword copyright © 2004 by George Grant

Cover design: Gore Studio, Inc.
Text design: Lisa Taylor

Library of Congress Cataloging-in-Publication Data
Morse, John Torrey, 1840-1937.
    Thomas Jefferson / John T. Morse, Jr. ; foreword by George Grant.
        p. cm. — (The American statesmen series)
    Reprint. Originally published: Boston : Houghton Mifflin, ©1898.
    Includes index.
    ISBN 1-58182-409-2 (pbk. : alk. paper)
    1. Jefferson, Thomas, 1743-1826. 2. Presidents—United States—Biography. I. Title. II. American statesmen series (Nashville, Tenn)
    E332.M84 2004
    973.4'6'092—dc22
                                                                      2004020901

Printed in the United States of America
1 2 3 4 5 6 7 8 — 09 08 07 06 05 04

★ CONTENTS ★

MORSE'S THOMAS JEFFERSON
By George Grant

THOMAS JEFFERSON WAS a complex and brilliant man who was practically born into America's ruling elite. He had served in the Virginia House of Burgesses, in the Continental Congress, as ambassador to the French court, as governor of Virginia, as secretary of state under George Washington, vice president under John Adams, and finally as president in his own right. He was the author of the Declaration of Independence. He was the founder of the University of Virginia. He established the Library of Congress. But despite all these credentials, Jefferson was hardly considered a member of the establishment. Indeed, he was best known as a revolutionary populist. When he won the presidential election of 1800, it was dubbed a kind of "bloodless revolution." He brought to the presidency his philosophy of representative government firmly rooted in the rights and liberties of individuals. As a result, he helped to dramatically change the character of the United States.

Jefferson's story, his life of stunning accomplishment, his radical Republican ideas, and his impact upon the young nation he had helped to found was the perfect centerpiece for the American Statesmen Series—a library of biographies first published on the threshold of the twentieth century in an effort to restore the very ideals Jefferson had stood for and fought for all his life.

John Torrey Morse (1840–1937) was the author of the volume

on Jefferson as well as the editor of the series. He was born into a prominent family of Boston Brahmins and graduated from Harvard in 1860. Two years later he was admitted to the Massachusetts bar and began to practice law. But, like Jefferson, Morse had wide-ranging interests. He was a lecturer in history at his alma mater. He served in the state legislature. He wrote widely on public policy, economics, and social theory. With Henry Cabot Lodge he served as editor of the *International Review*.

While at Harvard, he had become enthralled with the idea of recovering the old ideals of Jefferson and the other Founding Fathers. That passion had been largely instilled in him by the lectures of Henry Brooks Adams (1838–1918). Adams had long been an influential voice at Harvard, serving as an adjunct lecturer in history off and on since 1858. But it was when he was appointed professor of medieval history in 1870 that he gained an especially ardent following among students, alumni, and faculty alike—among them, men such as Morse and Lodge as well as Theodore Roosevelt, W. G. Sumner, Edward Shepard, A. B. Magruder, John Stevens, and Moses Tyler. Over the course of the next few years Adams and his enthusiastic followers bucked the trend of the scholastic and scientific modernists, emphasizing instead a much more classical approach to moral philosophy. In the process he revolutionized both Harvard and the discipline of history.

Adams himself had been born into one of the nation's most prominent families—both his grandfather and great-grandfather had been presidents of the United States, and his father had been ambassador to England during the tumult of the Civil War. Adams saw himself as a conservative traditionalist championing the old Democratic and Republican ideals of the seventeenth- and eighteenth-century Founders. He was appalled by the corruption and bureaucratization of modern American politics and believed that freedom's only hope lay in retelling the story of liberty in a vibrant and fresh fashion for a whole new generation.

Thus, Adams sought to teach history as a means of preserving the practical lessons and profound legacies of the American experience without the petty prejudice of Humanistic fashions or the parsimonious preference of Enlightenment innovations. He wanted to avoid the trap of noticing everything that had gone unnoticed in the past while failing to notice all that the past deemed notable. He shunned the kind of modern epic that today is shaped primarily by the banalities of sterile mechanical scientism or the fancies of empty theater scenes rather than the realities of historical profundity.

He believed that the best sort of history is always a series of lively adventure stories—and thus should be told without the cumbersome intrusion of arcane academic rhetoric or truckloads of extraneous footnotes. History from that perspective, he thought, is a romantic moral drama in a world gone impersonally scientific; hence, it should be told with a measure of passion, unction, and verve. For him, the record of the ages is actually philosophy teaching by example—and because however social conditions may change, the great underlying qualities which make and save men and nations do not alter, it is the most important example of all.

Morse enlisted the help of Lodge and the other Harvard intellectuals who had been influenced by Adams and his classical view of moral philosophy to put together a whole series of new biographies of the American Founders and the succeeding generations of likeminded American patriots. Every major figure in the first century of American independence would be covered: from presidents like George Washington, John Adams, Thomas Jefferson, James Madison, James Monroe, John Quincy Adams, and Andrew Jackson to statesmen like Samuel Adams, Patrick Henry, Alexander Hamilton, John Marshall, Henry Clay, Gouverneur Morris, and Thomas Hart Benton. The series was immediately lauded by the critics and embraced by the reading public. Several of the volumes became blockbuster bestsellers and have in the intervening years been repeatedly reprinted. But perhaps more importantly, the books helped to usher in a new era of political and social reform, which enabled the still gangly, young American nation to become an undisputed world power and a beacon light of freedom to oppressed peoples everywhere.

The republication of these volumes just over a century later is a welcome opportunity to remind yet another new generation of leaders of the great story of liberty. At a time when our freedoms are both taken for granted and threatened as never before, I trust we will be able to recover the passion for truth that so animated Morse and Adams and the others lest all they worked for be igno-miniously lost.

Thomas Jefferson

CHAPTER I

YOUTH

LITTLE MORE THAN a century ago a civilized nation without an aristocracy was a pitiful spectacle scarcely to be witnessed in the world. The American colonists, having brought no dukes and barons with them to the rugged wilderness, fell in some sort under a moral compulsion to set up an imitation of the genuine creatures, and as their best makeshift in the emergency they ennobled in a kind of local fashion the richer Virginian planters. These gentlemen were not without many qualifications for playing the agreeable part assigned to them; they gambled recklessly over cards and at the horse-racings and cock-fightings which formed their chief pleasures; they caroused to excess at taverns and at each other's houses; they were very extravagant, very lazy, very arrogant, and fully persuaded of their superiority over their fellows, whom they felt it their duty and their privilege to direct and govern; they had large landed estates and preserved the custom of entailing them in favor of eldest sons; they were great genealogists, and steeped in family pride; they occupied houses which were very capacious and noted for unlimited hospitality, but which were also ill-kept and barren; they were fond of field-sports and were admirable horsemen; they respected the code of honor and quarrelled and let blood as gentlemen should; they were generous, courageous and high-spirited; a few of them were liberally educated and

well-read. We all know that, when the days of trial came, the
best of them were little inferior to the best men whose names
are to be found in the history of any people in the world;[*]
though when one studies the antecedents and social surround-
ings whence these noble figures emerged, it seems as if for once
men had gathered grapes from thorns, and figs from thistles.

Rather upon the outskirts than actually within the sacred limits of this charmed circle, Thomas Jefferson was born on April 13,
1743. The first American Jefferson was dimly supposed to have
immigrated from Snowdon, in Wales; such at least was the family
"tradition;" while the only thing certainly to be predicated concerning him is that he was one of the earliest settlers, having
arrived in Virginia before the Mayflower had brought the first cargo
of Puritans to the New England coast. Peter Jefferson, the father of
Thomas, gave the family its first impetus on the road towards
worldly success. He was a man of superb physique and of corre-
spondingly vigorous intellect and enterprising temper. In early life
he became very intimate with William Randolph of Tuckahoe; he
"patented" in the wilderness a thousand acres of land adjoining the
larger estate of Randolph, bought from his friend four hundred
acres more, paying therefor the liberal price of "Henry
Weatherbourne's biggest bowl of arrack punch," as is jovially nominated in the deed; and further cemented the alliance by marrying
William's cousin, Jane Randolph, in 1738. The distinction which
this infusion of patrician blood brought to the commoner
Jeffersonian stream was afterwards slightingly referred to by
Thomas Jefferson, who said, with a characteristic democratic sneer,
that his mother's family traced "their pedigree far back in England
and Scotland, to which let every one ascribe the faith and merit he
chooses."

---

*It should be remembered that by good rights neither Washington, Jefferson, nor even
Madison, before they became distinguished, would have been entitled to take rank in the
exclusive coterie of the best Virginian families.

Peter Jefferson's plantation, or more properly his farm, for it seems to have been largely devoted to the culture of wheat, lay on the Rivanna near its junction with the James, including a large extent of plain and some of the lower shoulders or spurs of the mountains known as the Southwest Range. He named it Shadwell, after the parish in London where his wife had been born; among its hills was that of Monticello, upon which in after years Thomas Jefferson built his house. Peter was colonel of his county and a member of the House of Burgesses, apparently a man of rising note in the colony. But in August, 1757, in the fiftieth year of what seemed a singularly vigorous life, he suddenly died, leaving Thomas only fourteen years old, with the advantages, however, of a comfortable property and an excellent family connection on the mother's side, so that it would be his own fault if he should not prosper well in the world.

Jefferson appears to have been sensibly brought up, getting as good an education as was, possible in Virginia and paying also due regard to his physical training. He grew to be a slender and sinewy, or as some preferred to say, a thin and raw-boned young man, six feet two and one half inches tall; with hair variously reported as red, reddish, and sandy, and with eyes mixed of gray and hazel. Certainly he was not handsome, and in order to establish his social attractiveness his friends fall back on "his countenance, so highly expressive of intelligence and benevolence," and upon his "fluent and sensible conversation" intermingled with a "vein of pleasantry." He is said to have improved in appearance as he grew older, and to have become "a very good-looking man in middle age, and quite a handsome old man."* He was athletic, fond of shooting, and a skilful and daring horseman even for a Virginian. He early developed a strong taste for music and fiddled assiduously for many years. By his own desire he entered William and Mary College in 1760 at the age of seventeen.

*Tucker's *Life of Jefferson*, i. 29.

He was now secure of every advantage possible for a young Virginian. The college was at Williamsburg, then the capital of the colony, and his relationship with the Randolphs made him free of the best houses.* A Scotch doctor, William Small, was Professor of Mathematics and temporarily also of Philosophy. He appears to have had a happy gift of instruction, and to have fired the mind of his pupil with a great zeal for learning. Jefferson afterward even said that the presence of this gentleman at the University was "what probably fixed the destinies of my life."

If we may take Jefferson's own word for it, he habitually studied, during his second collegiate year, fifteen hours a day, and for his only exercise ran, at twilight, a mile out of the city and back again. Long afterward, in 1808, he wrote to a grandson a sketch of this period of his life, composed in his moral and didactic vein; in it he draws a beautiful picture of his own precocious and unnatural virtue, and is himself obliged to gaze in surprise upon one so young and yet so good amid crowding temptations. Without fully sharing in this generous admiration, we must not doubt that he was sufficiently studious and sensible, for he had a natural thirst for information and he always afterward appeared a broadly educated man. His preference was for mathematics and natural philosophy, studies which he deemed "so peculiarly engaging and delightful as would induce every one to wish an acquaintance with them." He was fond also of classics, and indeed eschewed with positive distaste no branch of study save only ethics and metaphysics. At these he sneered, and actually once had the courage to say that it was "lost time" to attend lectures on moral philosophy, since "he who made us would have been a pitiful

---

*But one must not draw too glowing a picture of the advantage of living in Williamsburg, which in fact was a village containing about two hundred houses, "one thousand souls, whites and negroes," and "ten or twelve gentlemen's families constantly residing in it, besides merchants and tradesmen." Only during the winter session of the legislature it became "crowded with the gentry of the country." See Parton's *Life of Jefferson*, 20.

bungler if he had made the rules of our moral conduct a matter of science." Certainly morals never became in his mind one of the exact sciences, and the heretical notion of his youth remained the conviction of his mature years. He appears to have read quite extensively, with sound selection and liberal taste, among the acknowledged classics in Greek, Latin, and English literature, and to some extent also in French and Italian. But novels he never fancied and rarely touched at any period of his life, though not by reason of a severe taste, since for a long while he was nothing less than infatuated with the bombast of Ossian.

After graduation, Jefferson read law in the office of George Wythe, a gentleman, whose genial social qualities and high professional attainments are attested by the friendly allusions of many eminent contemporaries.* His zeal in labor still continued, and again the story is told that he habitually reached the measure of fifteen hours of study daily. When he was about twenty-one years old, Jefferson drew up a plan of study and reading for a young friend: Before eight o'clock in the morning this poor fellow was to devote himself to "physical studies"; eight to twelve o'clock, law; twelve to one, politics; afternoon, history; "dark to bedtime," literature, oratory, etc., etc. Yet there were cakes and ale in those days, young girls and dancing at the Raleigh tavern, cards and horses; and the young Virginians had their full share of all these good things: Probably the fifteen hours stint, as a strictly regular daily allowance, is fabulous. With Professor Small and Mr. Wythe the young student formed a "partie quarrée" at the "palace" of Francis Fauquier, then the gay, agreeable, accomplished, free-thinking, gambling Governor of Virginia. The four habitually dined together in spite of the fifteen-hour rule, and it betokens no small degree of intellectual maturity on the part of Jefferson, that while a mere college lad he was the selected companion of three such gentlemen.

---

*John Marshall read law with him, and Henry Clay was his private secretary.

Fortunately his sound common sense protected him from the dangerous elements in the association.

A few letters written by Jefferson at this time to his friend John Page, a member of the well-known Virginian family of that name and himself afterward Governor of Virginia, have been preserved. Without showing much brilliancy, they abound in labored attempts at humor and are thickly sown with fragments from the classics and simple bits of original Latinity. The chief burden of them all is the girls, whose faces, it is to be hoped, were prettier than their names,—Sukey Potter, Judy Burwell, and the like. One of them, "Belinda," as he called her, he treated in a rather peculiar way. He told her that he loved her, but did not desire at present to engage himself, since he wished to go to Europe for an indefinite period; but he said that on his return, of course with unchanged affections, he would finally and openly commit himself. To this not very ardent proposition the lady naturally said No, and soon wedded another. The "laggard in love" wrote a despairing letter or two, which fail to bring tears to the reader's eyes; remained in comfortable bachelorhood a few short years, and then gave his hand, and doubtless also in all warmth and sincerity his heart, to the young widow of Bathurst Skelton. His marriage took place January 1, 1772. If the accounts of gallant chroniclers may be trusted, the bride had every qualification which can make woman attractive; an exquisite feminine beauty, grace of manners, loveliness of disposition, rare cleverness, and many accomplishments. Furthermore, her father, John Wayles, a rich lawyer, considerately died about sixteen months after the marriage, and so caused a handsome addition to Jefferson's property.

Jefferson, however, had no need to marry for money. Though not very rich, he was well off and was rapidly multiplying his assets. At the time of his marriage he had increased his patrimony so that 1,900 acres had swelled by purchases to 5,000 acres, and thirty slaves had increased to fifty-two. He was getting considerably upwards of $3,000 a year from his profession,* and $2,000 from his farm. This made a very good income in those days in Virginia. The evidence is abundant that he was thrifty, industrious, and successful. He seemed like one destined to accumulate wealth, but he never had a fair opportunity to show his capacity in this direction, since he maintained a resolve not to better his fortunes while in public life.

His career at the bar began in 1767, when he was only twenty-four years old, and closed in 1774. If he had only been getting fairly into business when he left the profession, he would have had little right to complain. But apparently he had stepped at once into an excellent practice, and either the chief occupation of all Virginians was litigation, or else he must have enjoyed exceptional good fortune. In the first year he had sixty eight cases in the "general court," in the next year one hundred and fifteen, in the third year one hundred and ninety-eight. Of causes before inferior tribunals no record was kept. Yet Mr. Randall tells us that he was chiefly an "office-lawyer," for that a husky weakness of the voice prevented him from becoming very successful as an advocate.

The farming, though it contributed the smaller fraction of his income, was the calling which throughout life he loved with an inborn fondness not to be quenched by all the cares and interests of a public career, and his notebooks attest the unresting interest which he brought to it in all times and places. A striking paper, unfortunately incomplete and undated, is published in the first volume of his works. "I sometimes ask myself," he writes, "whether my country is the better for my having lived at all. . . . I have been the instrument of doing the following things." Then are enumerated such matters as the disestablishment of the state church in Virginia, the putting an end to entails, the prohibition of the importation of slaves, also the drafting of the Declaration of

---

*During the seven years that he was in practice his fees averaged $3,000 per annum.

Independence, and in the same not very long list, cheek by jowl with these momentous achievements, follows the importation of olive plants from Marseilles into South Carolina and Georgia, and of heavy upland rice from Africa into the same States, in the hope that it might supersede the culture of the wet rice so pestilential in the summer. "The greatest service," he comments, "which can be rendered to any country is, to add a useful plant to its culture, especially a bread grain; next in value to bread is oil." At another time he wrote: "Those who labor in the earth are the chosen people of God, if ever he had a chosen people, whose breasts he has made his peculiar deposit fox substantial and genuine virtue. . . . Corruption of morals in the mass of cultivators is a phenomenon of which no age or nation has furnished an example. . . . Generally speaking, the proportion which the aggregate of the other classes of citizens bears in any state to that of the husbandmen is the proportion of its unsound to its healthy parts, and is a good enough barometer whereby to measure the degree of its corruption." From these premises he draws the conclusion that it is an error to attract artificers or mechanics from foreign parts into this country. It will be better and more wholesome, he says, to leave them in their European workshops and "carry provisions and materials to workmen there, than bring them to the provisions and materials, and with them their manners and principles." This would hardly pass nowadays for sound political economy; but it is an excellent sample of the simple impractical form into which Jefferson's reflections were apt to develop when the mood of dreamy virtue was upon him. During an inroad of yellow fever he found "consolation" in the reflection that Providence had so ordered things "that most evils are the means of producing some good. The yellow fever will discourage the growth of great cities in our nation, and I view great cities as pestilential to the morals, the health, and the liberties of man." Nor did wider experience of the world cause him to change his views. In 1785 he wrote from Paris: "Cultivators of the earth are the most valuable citizens. They are the most vigorous, the most independent, the most virtuous; and they are tied to their country and wedded to its liberty and interests by the most lasting bonds. . . . I consider the class of artificers as the panders of vice, and the instruments by which the liberties of a country are generally overturned." "Were I to indulge in my own theory," he again says, "I should wish them (the States) to practise neither commerce nor navigation, but to stand with respect to Europe precisely on the footing of China."

For his own personal part, Jefferson was always an enthusiast in agriculture. He was never too busy to find time to note the dates of the planting and the ripening of his vegetables and fruits. He left behind him a table enumerating thirty-seven esculents, and showing the earliest date of the appearance of each one of them in the Washington market in each of eight successive years. He had ever a quick observation and a keen intelligence ready for every fragment of new knowledge or hint of a useful invention in the way of field work. All through his busy official life, abroad and at home, he appears ceaselessly to have one eye on the soil and one ear open to its cultivators; he is always comparing varying methods and results, sending new seeds hither and thither, making suggestions, trying experiments, till, in the presence of his enterprise and activity, one begins to think that the stagnating character so commonly attributed to the Virginian planters must be fabulous. For, on the contrary, so far was his temperament removed from the conservatism of the Anglo-Saxon race that often he seemed to take the fact that a thing had never been done as a sufficient reason for doing it. All his tendencies were utilitarian. Though strangely devoid of any appreciation of fiction in literature, yet he had a powerful imagination, which ranged wholly in the unromantic domain of the useful, and ran riot in schemes for conferring practical benefits on mankind. He betrayed the same traits in agriculture and in politics. In both he was often a dreamer, but his dreams concerned the daily affairs of his fellow men, and his life was devoted to reducing his idealities to realities. It was largely this sanguine taste for novelty, this dash of the imaginative element, flavoring all his projects and doctrines, which made them attractive to the multitude, who, finding present facts to be for the most part hard and uninviting, are ever prone to be pleased with propositions for variety.

Only once, under the combined influences of Ossian, youth, and love, we find his fancy roving in a melodramatic direction. He turns then for a while from absorbing calculations of the amount of work which a man can do with a one-wheeled barrow and the amount he can do with a two-wheeled barrow, the number and cost of the nails required for a certain length of paling, the amount of lime, or limestone, required for a perch of stone wall, and in place of these useful computations he lays plans for ornamental work. He will "choose out for a burying place some unfrequented vale in the park," wherein a bubbling brook alone shall break the stillness, while around shall be "ancient and venerable oaks" interspersed with "gloomy evergreens." In the centre shall be a "small gothic temple of antique appearance." He will "appropriate one half to the use of his family," the other, with an odd manifestation of Virginian hospitality, to the use of "strangers," servants, etc. There shall be "pedestals, with urns and proper inscriptions" and a "pyramid of the rough rockstone" over the "grave of a favorite and faithful servant." There will be, of course, a grotto, "spangled with translucent pebbles and beautiful shells," with an ever trickling stream, a mossy couch, a figure of a sleeping nymph, and appropriate mottoes in English and Latin. It is needless to say that these idle fancies seem never to have been seriously taken in hand. More important and engrossing work than the preparation of an enticing grave-yard was forthwith to claim Jefferson's attention.

CHAPTER II

IN THE HOUSE OF BURGESSES

ABOUT THE TIME when he entered college, Jefferson made the acquaintance of Patrick Henry, then a rather unprosperous, hilarious, unknown young countryman, just admitted to the bar, though profoundly ignorant of law. An intimacy sprang up between them, and when Henry became a member of the House of Burgesses he often shared Jefferson's chambers at Williamsburg. From them he went, in May, 1765, to utter that ringing speech against taxation without representation which made him for a time foremost among Virginian patriots. In the doorway of the hall stood Jefferson, an entranced listener, thinking that Henry spoke "as Homer wrote." The magnetic influence of this brilliant friend would have transformed a more loyally disposed youth than Jefferson into an arrant rebel. But no influence was needed for this purpose; Jefferson was by nature a bold and free thinker, wanting rather ballast than canvas. As he watched the course of public events in those years when the germs of the Revolution were swelling and quickening in the land, all his sympathies were warmly enlisted with the party of resistance. By the year 1768, when the advent of a new governor made necessary the election of a new House of Burgesses, he already craved the opportunity to take an active part in affairs, and at once offered himself as a candidate for Albemarle County. He kept open house, distributed limitless punch, stood by the polls, politely bowing to every voter who named him, all according to the

Virginian fashion of the day,* and had the good fortune, by these meritorious efforts, to win success. On May 11, 1769, he took his seat. Lord Botetourt delivered his quasi-royal speech, and Jefferson drew the resolutions constituting the basis of the reply; but afterward, being deputed to draw the reply itself, he suffered the serious mortification of having his document rejected. On the third day the Burgesses passed another batch of resolutions, so odiously like a Bill of Rights that the Governor, much perturbed in his loyal mind, dissolved them at once. The next day they eked out this brief term of service by meeting in the "Apollo," or long room of the Raleigh tavern, where eighty-eight of them, of whom Jefferson was one, formed a non-importation league as against British merchandise. All the signers of this document were at once reëlected by their constituents.

In March, 1773, the Burgesses again came together in no good humor. The destruction of the Gaspee in Narragansett Bay had led to a draconic act of Parliament whereby any colonist, destroying so much as "the button of a mariner's coat," might be carried to England for trial and punished with death. Upon the assembling of the Burgesses, Jefferson and some five or six others, "not thinking our old and leading members up to the point of forwardness and zeal which the times required," met privately in consultation. The offspring of their conference was a standing committee charged to correspond with like committees which the sister colonies were invited to appoint. An idle controversy has arisen as to whether Massachusetts or Virginia was first to devise this system of correspondence. Jefferson long afterward averred that Virginia was the earlier, and the evidence favors the substantial correctness of his statement; for, though Massachusetts had suggested the idea some two years before, she had not pushed it, and the suggestion, known to few, had been forgotten by all. It naturally resulted from this pro-

---

*See Parton's description, in his *Life of Jefferson*, p. 88.

ceeding that the Burgesses were at once dissolved by the Earl of Dunmore. But the committee met on the next day and issued their circular of invitation.

A year later, in the spring of 1774, news of the Boston Port Bill came while the Burgesses were in session. Again Jefferson and some half dozen more, feeling that "the lead in the House on these subjects [should] no longer be left with the old members," and agreeing that they "must boldly take an unequivocal stand in the line with Massachusetts,"* met in secret to devise proper measures. They determined to appoint a day of fasting and prayer, and in the House they succeeded in carrying a resolution to that effect. Again the Governor dissolved them; again they went over to the "Apollo," and again passed there most disloyal resolutions. Among these was one requesting the Committee of Correspondence to consult the other colonies on the expediency of holding annually a general Congress; also another, for the meeting of representatives from the counties of Virginia in convention at Williamsburg on August 1. The freeholders of Albemarle elected Jefferson again a Burgess, and also a deputy to this Convention.

Jefferson started to attend the meeting of the Convention, but upon the road was taken so ill with a dysentery that he could not go on. He therefore forwarded a draft of instructions, such as he hoped to see given by that body to the delegates whom it was to send to the General Congress of the colonies. One copy of this document was sent to Patrick Henry, who, however, "communicated it

---

*The march of events, Jefferson afterward wrote, "favored the bolder spirits of Henry, the Lees, Pages, Mason, etc., with whom I went at all points. Sensible, however, of the importance of unanimity among our constituents, although we often wished to have gone faster, we slackened our pace that our less ardent colleagues might keep up with us; and they on their part, differing nothing from us in principle, quickened their gait somewhat beyond that which their prudence might, of itself, have advised, and thus consolidated the phalanx which breasted the power of Britain. By this harmony of the bold with the cautious, we advanced with our constituents, in undivided mass, and with fewer examples of separation than, perhaps, existed in any other part of the Union."

to nobody;" perhaps, says Jefferson, "because he disapproved the ground taken," perhaps "because he was too lazy to read it." Another copy was sent with better fortune to Peyton Randolph, President of the Convention. It was laid by him upon the table, was read by the members, and was so well liked that it was printed in pamphlet form under the title of "A Summary View of the Rights of British America;" in this shape it was sent over to Great Britain, was there "taken up by the opposition, interpolated a little by Mr. Burke," and then extensively circulated, running "rapidly through several editions."

Naturally that was the era of manifestoes in the colonies, and many pens were busy preparing documents, public and private, famous and neglected, but nearly all sound, spirited, generalizing, and declamatory. Jefferson's instructions did not wholly escape the prevalent faults, and had their share of rodomontade about the rights of freemen and the oppressions of monarchs. But these were slight blemishes in a paper singularly radical, audacious, and well argued. The migration of the "Saxon ancestors" of the present English people, he said, had been made "in like manner with that of the British immigrants to the American colonies."

> Nor was ever any claim of superiority or dependence asserted over [the English] by that Mother Country from which they had migrated; and were such a claim made, it is believed his Majesty's subjects in Great Britain have too firm a feeling of the rights derived to them from their ancestors, to bow down the sovereignty of their State before such visionary pretensions. And it is thought that no circumstance has occurred to distinguish materially the British from the Saxon emigration. America was conquered and her settlements made and firmly established at the expense of individuals, and not of the British public.

This was laying the axe at the very root of the tree with tolerable force; and more blows of the same sort followed. The connection undeniably existing between the colonies and the mother country was reduced to a minimum by an ingenious explanation. The emigrants, Jefferson said, had "thought proper" to "continue their union with England" "by submitting themselves to the same sovereign," who was a "central link" or "mediatory power" between "the several parts of the Empire," so that "the relation between Great Britain and these colonies was exactly the same as that of England and Scotland after the accession of James and until the union, and the same as her present relations with Hanover, having the same executive chief, but no other necessary connection." The corollary was "that the British Parliament has no right to exercise authority over us," and when it endeavored to do so "one free and independent legislature" took upon itself "to suspend the powers of another, free and independent as itself."

These were revolutionary words, and fell short by ever so little of that direct declaration of independence which they anticipated by less than two years. They would have cost Jefferson his head had it been less inconvenient to bring him to Westminster Hall, and even that inconvenience would probably have been overcome had forcible opposition been a little longer deferred in the colonies. As it was, the pamphlet "procured him the honor of having his name inserted in a long list of proscriptions enrolled in a bill of attainder commenced in one of the Houses of Parliament, but suppressed in embryo by the hasty step of events, which warned them to be a little cautious."

One can hardly be surprised that this Jeffersonian "leap was too long, as yet, for the mass of our citizens," and that "tamer sentiments were preferred" by the Convention. Jefferson himself frankly admitted, many years afterward, that the preference was wise. But his colleagues so well liked a boldness somewhat in excess of their own, that six months later, in view of the chance of

Peyton Randolph being called away from service in the Colonial Congress, they elected Jefferson as a deputy to fill the vacancy in case it should occur. Not many weeks later it did occur. But Jefferson was detained for a short time in order to draw the reply of the Burgesses to the celebrated "conciliatory proposition," or so called "olive branch," of Lord North. Otherwise it was "feared that Mr. Nicholas, whose mind was not yet up to the mark of the times," would undertake it. On June 10, 1775, the Burgesses accepted Jefferson's draft "with long and doubtful scruples from Nicholas and Mercer," only making some slight amendments which Jefferson described as "throwing a dash of cold water on it here and there, enfeebling it somewhat." The day after its passage Jefferson set forth to take his seat in Congress, bearing with him the document, which had been anxiously expected by that body as being the earliest reply from any colony to the ministerial proposition. Its closing paragraph referred the matter for ultimate action to the General Congress.

CHAPTER III

IN CONGRESS

JEFFERSON ARRIVED IN Philadelphia on the tenth day of his journey, and on June 21 became one of that assembly concerning which Lord Chatham truly said that its members had never been excelled "in solidity of reasoning, force of sagacity, and wisdom of conclusion." Jefferson, at the age of thirty-two, was among the younger deputies* in a body which, by the aid of Dr. Franklin, aged seventy-one, and Edward Rutledge, aged twenty-six, represented all the adult generations of the country. He brought with him a considerable reputation as a ready and eloquent writer, and was justly expected, by his counsel, his pen, and his vote, to bring substantial reinforcement to the more advanced party. In debate, however, not much was to be anticipated from him, for he was never able to talk even moderately well in a deliberative body. Not only was his poor voice an impediment, but he was a man who instinctively abhorred contest. Daringly as he wrote, yet he shrank from that contention which pitted him face to face against another, though the only weapons were the "winged words" of parliamentary argumentation. Turmoil and confusion he detested; amid wrangling and disputing he preferred to be silent; it was in conversation, in the committee-room, and preëminently when he had

---

*Not, as he himself with wonted inaccuracy says, "the youngest man but one;" for besides Edward Rutledge, born in 1749, there was also John Jay, born in 1745.

pen, ink, and paper before him, that he amply justified his presence among the three-score chosen ones of the thirteen colonies.
In his appropriate department he quickly superseded Jay as docu-
ment-writer to Congress.

Yet his first endeavor did not point to this distinction. When
news of the fight at Bunker's Hill arrived in Philadelphia, Congress
felt obliged to publish a manifesto setting before the world the justification of this now bloody rebellion. Jefferson, as a member of
the committee, undertook to draw the paper; but he made it much
too vigorous for the conciliatory and anxious temper of Dickinson;
so that partly out of regard for this courteous and popular gentleman, partly from a politic desire not to outstrip too far the slower
ranks, Jefferson's sheets were submitted to Dickinson himself for
revision. Not content with modification, that reluctant patriot prepared an entire substitute which was reported and accepted. But its
closing four and one half clauses were borrowed from the draft of
Jefferson, whose admirers think that these alone save the document from being altogether feeble and inadequate. Among them
were the following significant words: "We mean not to dissolve that
union which has so long and so happily subsisted between us, and
which we sincerely wish to see restored. Necessity has not yet
[note the pregnant word] driven us into that desperate measure."*

A month afterward Jefferson had better luck with his composition. He was second on the committee—of which the members
were chosen by ballot and took rank according to the number of
votes received by them respectively—deputed to draw the reply of
Congress to Lord North's "conciliatory proposition." He based his

---

*The authorship of these closing paragraphs has been denied to Jefferson and attributed to
Dickinson. But the evidence would establish only a small measure of probability in favor of
Dickinson, if it stood wholly uncontradicted; and it utterly fails to meet and control
Jefferson's direct assertion, made in his Autobiography, p. 11, that these words were retained
from his own draft. The anxiety to claim them for Dickinson shows the comparative estima-
tion in which they are held. See *Magazine of Amer. Hist.* viii. 514.

paper on the reply already drawn by him for the Virginian Burgesses, and was gratified by seeing it readily accepted. A few days later Congress adjourned, and Jefferson resumed his seat and duties in the State Convention, by which he was at once reëlected to Congress, this time standing third on the list of delegates.

Much time has been wasted in idle efforts to determine precisely when and by whom the idea of separation and consequent independence of the provinces was first broached before the Colonial Congress. The inquiry is useless for many reasons, but conclusively so because all the evidence which the world is ever likely to see has been already adduced and has not sufficed to remove the question out of the domain of discussion. The truth is that while no intelligent man could help contemplating this probable conclusion, all deprecated it, many with more of anxiety than resolution, but not a few with a more daring spirit. In varying moods even the same individual might have different feelings. In his habitual frame of mind Jefferson thought separation to be daily approaching, and in the near presence of so momentous an event he was so far grave and dubious as to express a strong disinclination for it, though avowedly preferring it with all its possible train of woes to a continuance of the present oppression. He was too thoughtful not to be a reluctant revolutionist, but for the same reason he was sure to be a determined one. His relative, John Randolph, Attorney-General of the colony, was a loyalist, and in the summer of 1775 was about to remove to England. Jefferson wrote to him a friendly, serious letter, suggesting some considerations which he hoped that Randolph might have opportunity to lay before the English government, advantageously for both parties. He deprecates the present "contention" and the "continuance of confusion," which for him constitute, "of all states but one, the most horrid." He says that England

> would be certainly unwise, by trying the event of
> another campaign, to risk our accepting a foreign aid,

which perhaps may not be obtainable but on condition of everlasting avulsion from Great Britain. This would be thought a hard condition to those who still wish for a re-union with their parent country. I am sincerely one of those, and would rather be in dependence on Great Britain, properly limited, than on any other nation on earth, or than on no nation. But I am one of those, too, who, rather than submit to the rights of legislating for us assumed by the British Parliament, and which late experience has shown they will so cruelly exercise, would lend my hand to sink the whole island in the ocean.

This was written August 25, 1775; three months later he wrote, with a perceptible increase of feeling: —

It is an immense misfortune to the whole empire to have a king of such a disposition at such a time. . . . In an earlier part of this contest our petitions told him that from our King there was but one appeal. The admonition was despised and that appeal forced on us. To undo his empire, he has but one truth more to learn,—that, after colonies have drawn the sword, there is but one step more they can take. That step is now pressed upon us by the measures adopted, as if they were afraid we would not take it. Believe me, dear sir, there is not in the British Empire a man who more cordially loves a union with Great Britain than I do. But by the God that made me, I will cease to exist before I yield to a connection on such terms as the British Parliament propose; and in this I think I speak the sentiments of America. We want neither inducement nor power to declare and assert a separation. It is will alone that is wanting, and that is growing apace under the fostering hand of our King. One bloody campaign will probably decide, everlastingly, our future course; and I am sorry to find a bloody campaign is decided on.

In the autumn of 1775 Jefferson was again attending Congress in Philadelphia; early in 1776 he came home; but on May 13, 1776, he was back in his seat as a delegate from the Colony, soon to be the State, of Virginia. Events, which ten years ago had begun a sort of glacial movement, slow and powerful, were now advancing fast. On this side of the Atlantic, Thomas Paine had sent "Common Sense" abroad among the people, and had stirred them profoundly. Since the bloodshed at Lexington and Charlestown, Falmouth had been burned, Norfolk bombarded, and General Washington, concluding triumphantly the leaguer around Boston, was as open and efficient an enemy of England as if he had been a Frenchman or a Spaniard. It was time to transmute him from a rebel into a foreigner. Nor had the members of Congress any chance of escaping the hangman's rope unless this alteration could be accomplished for all the colonists. For all prominent men, alike in military and in civil life, it was now independence or destruction. Virginia instructed her delegates to move that Congress should declare "the United Colonies, free and independent States," and on June 7 Richard Henry Lee offered resolutions accordingly. In debate upon these on June 8 and 10 it appeared, says Jefferson, that certain of the colonies "were not yet matured for falling from the parent stem, but that they were fast advancing to that state." To give the laggards time to catch up with the vanguard, further discussion was postponed until July 1. But to prevent loss of time, when debate should be resumed, Congress on June 11 appointed a committee charged to prepare a Declaration of Independence, so that it might be ready at once when it should be wanted. The members, in the order of choice by ballot, were: Thomas Jefferson, John Adams, Benjamin Franklin, Roger Sherman, and Robert R. Livingston.

For the last hundred years one of the first facts taught to any child of American birth is, that Jefferson wrote the Declaration of Independence. The original draft in his handwriting was afterward deposited in the State Department. It shows two or three trifling alterations, interlined in the handwritings of Franklin and Adams. Otherwise it came before Congress precisely as Jefferson wrote it. Many years afterward John Adams gave an account of the way in which Jefferson came to be the composer of this momentous document, differing slightly from the story told by Jefferson. But the variance is immaterial, hardly greater than any experienced lawyer would expect to find between the testimony of two honest witnesses to any transaction, especially when given after the lapse of many years, and when one at least had no memoranda for refreshing his memory. Jefferson's statement seems the better entitled to credit, and what little corroboration is to be obtained for either narrator is wholly in his favor. He says simply that when the Committee came together he was pressed by his colleagues unanimously to undertake the draft; that he did so; that, when he had prepared it, he submitted it to Dr. Franklin and Mr. Adams, separately, requesting their corrections, "which were two or three only and merely verbal," "interlined in their own handwritings;" that the report in this shape was adopted by the committee, and a "fair copy," written out by Mr. Jefferson, was then laid before Congress.

A somewhat more interesting discussion concerns the question, how Jefferson came to be named first on the committee, to the entire exclusion of Lee, to whom, as mover of the resolution, parliamentary etiquette would have assigned the chairmanship. Many explanations have been given, of which some at least appear the outgrowth of personal likings and dislikings. It is certain that Jefferson was not only preëminently fitted for the very difficult task of this peculiar composition, but also that he was a man without an enemy. His abstinence from any active share in debate had saved him from giving irritation; and it is a truth not to be concealed, that there were cabals, bickerings, heart-burnings, perhaps actual enmities among the members of that famous body, which, grandly as it looms up, and rightly too, in the mind's eye, was after all composed of jarring human ingredients. It was well believed that there was a faction opposed to Washington, and it was generally suspected that irascible, vain, and jealous John Adams, then just rising from the ranks of the people, made in this matter common cause with the aristocratic Virginian Lees against their fellow-countryman. Adams frankly says that he himself was very unpopular; and therefore it did not help Lee to be his friend. Furthermore, the anti-Washingtonians were rather a clique or faction than a party, and were greatly outnumbered. Jay, too, had his little private pique against Lee. So it is likely enough that a timely illness of Lee's wife was a fortunate excuse for passing him by, and that partly by reason of admitted aptitude, partly because no risk could be run of any interference of personal feelings in so weighty a matter, Jefferson was placed first on the committee with the natural result of doing the bulk of its labor.

On July 1, pursuant to assignment, Congress, in committee of the whole, resumed consideration of Mr. Lee's resolution, and carried it by the votes of nine colonies. South Carolina and Pennsylvania voted against it. The two delegates from Delaware were divided. Those from New York said that personally they were in favor of it and believed their constituents to be so, but they were hampered by instructions drawn a twelvemonth since and strictly forbidding any action obstructive of reconciliation, which was then still desired. The committee reported, and then Edward Rutledge moved an adjournment to the next day, when his colleagues, though disapproving the resolution, would probably join in it for the sake of unanimity. This motion was carried, and on the day following the South Carolinians were found to be converted; also a third member "had come post from the Delaware counties" and caused the vote of that colony to be given with the rest;

Pennsylvania changed her vote; and a few days later the Convention of New York approved the resolution, "thus supplying the void occasioned by the withdrawing of her delegates from the vote."

On the same day, July 2, the House took up Mr. Jefferson's draft of the Declaration, and debated it during that and the following day and until a late hour on July 4. Many verbal changes were made, most of which were conducive to closer accuracy of statement, and were improvements. Two or three substantial amendments were made by the omission of passages; notably there was stricken out a passage in which George III was denounced for encouraging the slave-trade. It was thought disingenuous to attack him for tolerating a traffic conducted by Northern ship-owners and sustained by Southern purchasers, though it was true that sundry attempts of the Southern colonies to check it by legislation had been brought to naught by the king's refusal or neglect to ratify the enactments. Congress also struck out the passage in which Jefferson declared that the hiring of foreign mercenaries by the English must "bid us renounce, forever these unfeeling brethren," and cause us to "endeavor to forget our former love for them, and hold them as we hold the rest of mankind, enemies in war, in peace friends." It was thought better to say nothing which could be construed as an animadversion on the English people. No interpolation of any consequence was made.

Jefferson had ample cause to congratulate himself upon this event of the discussion. While it was in progress and his paper was undergoing sharp criticism during nearly three days, he felt far from cheerful. He himself spoke not a word in the debate, partly, perhaps, from a sense of incapacity to hold his own in so strenuous a contest of tongues, but also deeming it a "duty to be . . . a passive auditor of the opinions of others, more impartial judges." Dr. Franklin sat by him, and, seeing him "writhing a little under the acrimonious criticisms on some of its parts," told him, "by way of comfort," the since famous story of the sign of John Thompson, the hatter. The burden of argument, from which Jefferson wisely shrank, was gallantly borne by John Adams, whom Jefferson gratefully called "the colossus of that debate." Jefferson used afterward to take pleasure in tingeing the real solemnity of the occasion with a coloring of the ludicrous. The debate, he said, seemed as though it might run on interminably and probably would have done so at a different season of the year. But the weather was oppressively warm and the room occupied by the deputies was hard by a stable, whence the hungry flies swarmed thick and fierce, alighting on the legs of the delegates and biting hard through their thin silk stockings. Treason was preferable to discomfort, and the members voted for the Declaration and hastened to the table to sign it and escape from the horse-fly. John Hancock, making his great familiar signature, jestingly said that John Bull could read that without spectacles; then, becoming more serious, began to impress on his comrades the necessity of their "all hanging together in this matter." "Yes, indeed," interrupted Franklin, "we must all hang together, or assuredly we shall all hang separately." "When it comes to the hanging," said Harrison, the "luxurious heavy gentleman" from Virginia, to the little meagre Gerry of Massachusetts, "I shall have the advantage of you; it will be all over with me, long before you have done kicking in the air." Amid such trifling, concealing grave thoughts, Jefferson saw his momentous document signed at the close of that summer afternoon; he had acted as undertaker for the royal colonies and as midwife for the United States of America.

It is a work of supererogation to criticise a paper with which fifty millions of people are today as familiar as with the Lord's Prayer. The faults which it has are chiefly of style and are due to the spirit of those times, a spirit bold, energetic, sensible, independent, in action the very best but in talk and writing much too tolerant of broad and high sounding generalization. John Adams and Pickering long afterward, when they had come to hate

Jefferson as a sort of political arch-fiend, blamed it for lack of originality. Every idea in it, they said, had become "hackneyed" and was to be found in half a dozen earlier expressions of public opinion. The assertion was equally true, absurd, and malicious. No intelligent man could suppose that the Americans had been concerned in a rebellious discussion for years, and engaged in actual war for months, without having fully comprehended the principles, the causes, and the justification on which their conduct was based. It was preposterous to demand new discoveries in these particulars. Had such been possible, they would have been undesirable; it would have been extreme folly for Jefferson to open new and unsettling discussions at this late date. Of this charge against his production Jefferson said, with perfect wisdom and fairness, "I did not consider it as any part of my charge to invent new ideas altogether and to offer no sentiment which had ever been expressed before."

The statement that all men are created "equal" has been declared liable to misconstruction; but no intelligent man has ever misconstrued it, unless intentionally. So the criticism may be disregarded as trivial. Professor Tucker justly remarks of the whole paper that it is "consecrated in the affections of Americans, and praise may seem as superfluous as censure would be unavailing."

CHAPTER IV

AGAIN IN THE HOUSE OF BURGESSES

JEFFERSON WAS REËLECTED to Congress on June 20, 1776, but declined to serve. At the time he assigned as his reason "the situation of his domestic affairs" and "private causes," into which "the delicacy of the House would not require him to enter minutely." Many years afterward he declared a different motive: "When I left Congress, in 1776, it was in the persuasion that our whole code must be reviewed and adapted to our republican form of government, and now that we had no negative of councils, governors, and kings, to restrain us from doing right, that it should be corrected in all its parts, with a single eye to reason and the good sense of those for whose government it was framed." "I knew that our legislation, under the regal government, had many very vicious points which urgently required reformation, and I thought I could be of more use in forwarding that work."

The ex-colonies reorganized themselves in the shape of independent states very readily. On August 13, 1777, Jefferson wrote to Franklin that, "with respect to the State of Virginia . . . the people seemed to have laid aside the monarchical, and taken up the republican, government with as much ease as would have attended their throwing off an old and putting on a new suit of clothes. We are at present in the complete and quiet exercise of well-organized government." Times which made this transfiguration so easy were naturally ripe for other changes also. It was the era of revolution, of destruction and re-creation, in orderly fashion to be sure, so far as possible; but still the temper of the hour was favorable for a general revision of all the established laws and forms of society. The people were like a ploughed field in which the political sower might scatter broadcast new ideas and innovating doctrines with fair hope of an early harvest. Jefferson, reformer and radical by nature, instinctively knew his opportunity and went forth zealously to this task. Certainly he cast strong and wholesome seed, and with liberal hand, into the ready social furrows around him. Much of his planting struck root at once; much more lay in the ground for a long period, so that it was ten years before some of the bills introduced by him during the two years of his service were actually passed into laws; only a little unfortunately never fructified. The results of his labor changed not only the surface but the fundamental strata of the social and economical system of Virginia. Of course he did not accomplish so much without assistance. George Mason, George Wythe, and Madison, then a "new member and young," were efficient coadjutors. But they were coadjutors and lieutenants only; Jefferson was the principal and the leader.

On October 7, 1776, he took his seat in the House of Delegates and at once was placed on many committees. On October 11 he obtained leave to bring in a bill establishing Courts of Justice throughout the new State. On the next day he obtained leave to bring in a bill to enable tenants in tail to convey entailed property in fee simple. Two days later he reported a bill doing away with the whole system of entail. It was an audacious move. From generation to generation lands and slaves—almost the only valuable kind of property in Virginia—had been handed down protected against creditors, even against the very extravagance of spendthrift owners; and it was largely by this means that the quasi-nobility of the colony had succeeded in establishing and maintaining itself. A great groan seemed to go up from all respectable society at the terrible suggestion of Jefferson, a suggestion daringly cast before an

Assembly thickly sprinkled with influential delegates strongly bound by family ties and self-interest to defend the present system. Records of the times fail to explain the sudden and surprising success of a reform, which there was every reason to suppose could be carried through only very slowly and by desperate contests; we know little more than the strange fact that the whole system of entail in Virginia crashed to pieces almost literally in a day, carrying with it an "aristocracy" somewhat brummagem, but the only one which has ever existed in the territory now of the United States.

The cognate principle of primogeniture followed, assailed by the same vigorous hand. At least, implored Pendleton, if the eldest son may no longer inherit all the lands and the slaves of his father, let him take a double share. No, said Jefferson, the leveller, not till he can eat a double allowance of food and do a double allowance of work. So an equal distribution of property was established among the children of intestates; and though by will any one might still prefer an eldest son, yet the effect of the law upon public opinion was so great that all distinctions of this kind rapidly faded away.

Thus was a great social revolution wrought in a few months by one man. In his grandiose, humanitarian, self-laudatory vein, Jefferson afterward wrote that his purpose was, "instead of an aristocracy of wealth, of more harm and danger than benefit to society, to make an opening for the aristocracy of virtue and talent, which nature has wisely provided for the direction of the interests of society, and scattered with equal hand through all its conditions." But his brilliant triumph cost him a price. That distinguished class, whose existence as a social caste had been forever destroyed, reviled the destroyer from this time forth with relentless animosity; and, even to the second and third generations, the descendants of many of these patrician families vindictively cursed the statesman who had placed them on a level with the rest of their countrymen.

Jefferson's next important assault was upon the Established Church. Jefferson's religious views have given no small trouble to his biographers, who have been at much pains to make him out a sound Christian in the teeth of many charges of free-thinking. There is little evidence to show what his belief was at this period of his life. Certainly he did not flout or openly reject, Christianity; not improbably he had a liberal tolerance for its tenets rather than any profound faith in them. On August 10, 1787, in a letter of advice to his young ward, Peter Carr, he dwelt upon religion at much length, telling Carr to examine the question independently. He added instructions so colorless that they resemble the charge of a painfully impartial judge to a jury. But in this especial matter labored impartiality usually signifies a negative prejudice. At least Jefferson showed that he did not regard Christianity as so established a truth that it was to be asserted dogmatically, and though he so carefully seeks to conceal his own bias, yet one instinctively feels that this letter was not written by a believer. Had he believed, in the proper sense of the word, he would have been unable to place a very young man midway between the two doors of belief and unbelief, setting both wide open, and furnishing no indication as to which led to error. Yet as any inference may possibly be wrong, it is perhaps safer to admit that the problem of his present faith or unfaith is not surely soluble, and to rest content with saying—what alone is now necessary—that he certainly viewed with just abhorrence the mediaeval condition of religious legislation in Virginia in 1777.

He set about the task of clearing away this dead wood no less vigorously and extensively than he had hewed at the obstructive social timbers. But, strange to say, the apparently sapless limbs gave the stouter resistance. He aimed at complete religious freedom, substantially such as now exists throughout the United States; but he was able only to induce a legislature, in which churchmen largely predominated, to take some initial steps in that direction. Yet the impetus which he gave, refreshed by others during a few succeeding years, at last brought the law-makers to the goal, so that in 1786 the full length of his reform was reached and his original "bill for establishing religious freedom" was passed, with immaterial amendments.

Here again it is to be said that Jefferson was in that position in which alone he ever won success; he was the mouthpiece of multitudes too numerous not to be heard, the leader of popular movement too massive to be obstructed. The majority of citizens were dissenters from the established Episcopal Church, and were resolved no longer to contribute of their funds for its support. Jefferson says that "the first republican legislature . . . was crowded with petitions to abolish this spiritual tyranny." This fact gave him the strength that he needed. He only required, but he always did require, that confidence and inspiration which came to him from the sense of having at his back largely superior numbers: it mattered not that they were ignorant, so that they were much the greater number. It is impossible to imagine Jefferson combating a popular error, controlling a mistaken people, encountering a great clamor of the masses. From these earliest days of his public career we find him always moving and feeling with the huge multitude, catching with sensitive ear the deep mutterings of its will, long before the inarticulate sound was intelligible to others in high places, encouraged by its later and hoarser outcry, gathering his force and power from its presence, his incentive and persistence from its laudation.

Almost immediately after taking his seat among the delegates, Jefferson had been placed at the head of a committee of five, charged with the general revision of all the laws of Virginia. It was an enormous task, of which he did much more than his just share. Some of the legislation referred to in the preceding pages found its place in the report of this committee. Other important matters, also included in the same report, can only be mentioned. The seat of government was removed from the commercial metropolis of Williamsburg to the small but central village of Richmond. The like principle has since prevailed in the selection of much the largest proportion of our state capitals. A bill for promoting the prompt naturalization of foreigners gave form to the subsequent practice of the country in this matter, and was only blameworthy because it failed to protect a large and easy admission by any checks of fitness in the way of knowledge and intelligence. Like much of Jefferson's work it was too democratic, as if all men must be fit for all things; also, like some of his work, it was not justified by his own principles declared at other times when his thoughts happened to be taking a different direction. A code of punishment for crime was drawn up, which was a vast improvement upon the merciless severity of preceding laws, but which retained to an unjustifiable extent and against the wishes of Jefferson the principle of retaliation. An elaborate school system was also devised; but the narrow prejudice of the rich planters prevented it from ever being fully adopted and properly set in working order.

As has been intimated, this mass of legislation, of which only the more prominent portions have been mentioned, was not all enacted during the two years of Jefferson's presence in the House of Delegates. Much of it, notably in the criminal department, lay untouched for a long time; but the laws reported by Jefferson formed a sort of reservoir from which the Legislature drew from time to time, during many following years, so much as they had leisure or inclination to use. It was not until the close of the Revolutionary War that leisure was found really to finish the whole business. But when at last the end was reached, few serious alterations had been made; and though it would be an exaggeration to assert that by 1786–87 the statute-book of Virginia had become a Jeffersonian code, yet it is within the truth to say that the impress of his mind was in every part of the volume, and that especially the social legislation was due chiefly to his influence.

Only in one grave matter—gravest, indeed, of all—he and a few humane and noble coadjutors encountered an utter defeat, which cost Virginia a great price of retribution in years thereafter. This concerned negro slavery. Though Jefferson did not, like his friend Wythe, emancipate his own slaves, yet from his early years he had been strongly opposed to slavery, as were many of the best and wisest Virginians of that day. Now the committee of revisers, pondering deeply on this difficult problem, and having it very much in their hearts to cleanse their State from a malady which they foresaw must otherwise prove fatal, contented themselves in the first instance with returning in their report a "mere digest of the existing laws . . . without any intimation of a plan for a future and general emancipation. It was thought better that this should be kept back, and attempted only by way of amendment, whenever the bill should be brought on. The principles of the amendment, however, were agreed on, that is to say, the freedom of all born after a certain day, and deportation at a proper age." But all this strategy was of no avail. "It was found that the public mind would not yet bear the proposition, nor will it bear it even to this day; yet," continues Jefferson, writing in his autobiography in 1821, "the day is not distant when it must bear and adopt it, or worse will follow. Nothing is more certainly written in the book of fate than that these people are to be free." How fortunate had it been for Virginia could she have been persuaded by the words spoken by her son, wise beyond his time, and by his fellow prophets in this great cause.

Yet when one examines Jefferson's scheme in its details, its primordial destiny of failure becomes at once evident. His project was as follows:—All negroes born of slave parents after the passing of the act were to be free, but to a certain age were to remain with their parents, and were "then to be brought up at the public expense to tillage, arts, or sciences, according to their geniuses, till the females should be eighteen and the males twenty-one years of age, when they should be colonized to such place as the circumstances of the time should render most proper, sending them out with arms, implements of household and of the handicraft arts, seeds, pairs of the useful domestic animals, etc." The United States were then "to declare them a free and independent people, and extend to them our alliance and protection, till they have acquired strength; and to send vessels at the same time to other parts of the world for an equal number of white inhabitants, to induce whom to migrate hither proper encouragements were to be proposed."

In the notion that such a costly and elaborate scheme might be carried into effect we get a manifestation of the most dangerous weakness of Jefferson's mind. His visionary tendency would thus often get the better of his shrewder sense, and the line of demarcation between the practicable and the impracticable would then become shadowy or wholly obliterated for him. In palliation it can only be remembered that he lived in an age of social and political theorizing, and that he was a man eminently characteristic of his era, sensitive to its influences and broadly reflecting its blunders not less than its wisdom.

Probably even at this early date the slavery problem had become insoluble. Certainly Jefferson's opinions concerning the two races in their possible relations towards each other rendered it insoluble by him. He also felt sure that "the two races, equally free, cannot live in the same government." The attempt, he predicted, would "divide Virginians into parties and produce convulsions which would probably never end but in the extermination of the one or the other race." Perhaps in this he was wrong. Yet holding these two firm convictions it is impossible to see what better plan he could have adopted than that which he did adopt, impossible though it was of execution. At least his prescience of a condition of things at which, as he said, "human nature must shudder," proves his social and political foresight.

One practical measure he did carry. Virginia, while still a colony, had made many efforts, rendered futile by royal obstruction, to stop the importation of slaves. In 1778, "in the very first session held under the republican government," Jefferson introduced a bill for this purpose which was readily passed without opposition. With this he was much and justly pleased, saying, "it will in some measure stop the increase of this great political and moral evil, while the minds of our citizens may be ripening for a complete emancipation of human nature." What he meant by this vague and absurd phrase, so characteristic of his habits of expression, it is not easy to say, and for the moment one almost forgets the high deserts of the reformer in irritation at his chatter about "the complete emancipation of human nature."

CHAPTER V

GOVERNOR OF VIRGINIA

PATRICK HENRY, FIRST Governor of the independent State of Virginia, served, by reëlections, three successive years, and was then, by the constitution, ineligible for another term. In January, 1779, the Legislature chose Jefferson to succeed him on the following June 1. The honor was not greatly to be coveted, yet Jefferson found a competitor for it in the friend of his youth, John Page, over whom he triumphed by a very few votes. The old good feeling between the two contestants was very creditably preserved throughout the political campaign, and perhaps by the time Jefferson left office he would have been glad if Page had been the successful candidate, and Page might rejoice at the opposite conclusion. For in this chapter of Jefferson's life the task of his biographers has been, to encounter the widespread impression that his administration was disgracefully inefficient. Mr. Randall especially has discussed this matter elaborately, and his facts and arguments, when rescued dripping from the sea of rhetoric and fine writing in which he nearly drowns them, appear to establish a satisfactory defence. Yet a man in public life does not achieve a complete success when he can be defended against charges of gross incompetency; and the negative assertion that Jefferson did not make a bad governor is by no means equivalent to the positive commendation that he made a really good one. The truth is, that he was not fitted to be a "war-governor," and though he did as well as he could, he did not do so well as some others might have done.

Until very nearly the close of Henry's third term, Virginia had enjoyed a happy immunity from invasion. Otherwise, however, she had borne her full share of patriotic burdens, and it may be imagined that the willing steed, spurred for three years by so hard a rider as Henry, was somewhat breathless and exhausted when he left the saddle. So, indeed, Jefferson found it. Men, horses, and food, Virginia had lavishly given; also arms and money, so far as she had been able. At last the point was close at hand at which further contributions involved such severe suffering that they must inevitably come slowly and reluctantly. Nevertheless Jefferson's sole business was to keep the stream still flowing and replenished. At first he was able to do surprisingly well. When he called for recruits for Greene's army in the Carolinas, many farmers came gallantly forward from the already sorely depleted fields. By September, 1780, there were not muskets for the men who were willing to march; neither a shilling in the treasury; wagons and horses could be had only by impressment, a hazardous pressure to put upon a people fighting for freedom. But it was inevitable, and it was applied to all alike; a wagon, a pair of horses, and two Negro drivers were taken from Governor Jefferson's own farm. A month later he hopes the new levies "will be all shod," and cannot say "what proportion will have blankets," though he is purchasing "every one which can be found out; there is a prospect of furnishing about half of them with tents."

It was a cruel blow, soon after, to learn that a large proportion of these scarce and valuable supplies were destroyed or captured, and that Cornwallis, with his face set northward, was leading a victorious army towards Virginia. It was an almost miraculous good fortune which checked his march a short distance from the border. But in the moment of apprehension Jefferson was bitterly blamed for having uselessly expended Virginian resources in Carolina. The accusation was grossly unjust. The Governor had been perfectly right in sending all the men and supplies he could muster to the places where the fighting was going forward. How else was the war to be maintained? What better course could be devised, not only for securing a general and ultimate success but also for keeping actual war at a distance from Virginia? The blunder would have been to send meagre supplies, and retain a still insufficient reserve at home, thus allowing the English to conquer in detail.

In another matter, more in his line, Jefferson again showed good judgment. The enterprising frontier fighter, General George Rogers Clarke, by a bold and soldierly movement in the far northwestern part of the State, captured the British Colonel Hamilton. This officer had been accused of many atrocities, and though the charges probably outran the truth, yet Jefferson was justified in believing him a guilty man.* He accordingly ordered the Colonel and two more officers to be put in irons and closely confined. The British General, Phillips, protested. Jefferson referred the matter to Washington, who, with much hesitation and apparent reluctance, advised a mitigation of the extreme severity. But the dose was wholesome and Jefferson's stern readiness to administer it had a salutary effect. He had in his keeping a large number of British prisoners, including many of high rank, and his avowed purpose, thus substantially enforced, to repay cruelty in kind and to retaliate hangings, irons, close confinement, and prison ships with identical measures upon his own part, undoubtedly checked the brutal tendencies of too many of the English officers.

Almost the last occurrence in Virginia under Governor Henry's administration had been a British raid. A dozen vessels landed some two thousand troops, who burned and ravaged extensively for a few days, wholly unmolested, and then returned as they had come. The affair was a dangerous indication to the English of the

---

*Professor Tucker in his *Life of Jefferson* undertakes to defend Hamilton. But his defence amounts to little or nothing more than that he knew Hamilton, and thought him quite too good a fellow and too much of a gentleman to have been guilty of the behavior alleged against him.

destruction which they could easily accomplish in this great reservoir of supplies. Yet it was not until late in October, 1780, that they repeated the enterprise. On the 22d of that month news came to Governor Jefferson that a fleet of sixty sail had anchored in Hampton Roads; four of the vessels were armed, while transports were putting on shore a land force roughly estimated at upwards of twenty-five hundred men. This was terrible intelligence in a thinly-settled country, where it must be long before an adequate defensive array could be assembled. Yet even men were more plentiful than muskets, and Jefferson sadly wrote: "it is mortifying to suppose that a people, able and zealous to contend with their enemy, should be reduced to fold their arms for want of the means of defence." Two or three weeks later "the prospect of arms" continued to be "very bad indeed." Moreover, in Albemarle County, hard by the anchorage ground, there were some four thousand prisoners of war, Burgoyne's army, who had been consigned to Virginia for safe-keeping. Cornwallis having lately defeated Gates badly at Camden, was less than one hundred and fifty miles from the Virginian border. A messenger from General Leslie, the commander of the invading body, was captured, having in his mouth a little quid containing a note to Cornwallis indicating a plan to unite both armies. In such imminent jeopardy the State and the Governor stood helpless, but ultimately were saved by good fortune and lack of enterprise on the part of the English. The North Carolina patriots harassed Cornwallis till he actually fell back to the southward. Leslie lay a month in camp, making no movement, then embarked and sailed away. Virginia had another surprising respite.

The third time the State was to fare worse. On the morning of Sunday, December 31, 1780, Jefferson again received intelligence that a fleet of twenty-seven vessels had entered Chesapeake Bay on the preceding day. Whatever may have been the case heretofore, it cannot be denied that he was now culpably remiss. It is true that he did not know that the fleet might not be French, or that its destination might not be Baltimore. But he did know that it certainly might be British, that its destination might be Williamsburg, Petersburg, or Richmond, and that in such event the best speed could not collect the Virginian levies rapidly enough. It was the dead of winter, not a severe season in Virginia, and when the husbandman is idle. It is impossible to suggest a satisfactory reason why Jefferson should not, in such probable and instant emergency, have prepared at once for the worst. He did not; he simply dispatched General Nelson, with abundant authority, to the lower river counties. Then he waited.

On Tuesday morning, fifty valuable but wasted hours after the first news reached him, he at last got definite information which showed him how stupid he had been. The fleet was hostile and was coming up the James. Then he did what he ought to have done at eight o'clock a.m. of the preceding Sunday; he ordered out forty-seven hundred militia-men from the nearest counties. Furthermore, having at last got fairly at work, he showed considerable personal energy. He got the public papers and some stores and articles of value across the river to a less exposed place, and he galloped about the country terribly busy and excited, till he killed his horse and was obliged to mount an unbroken colt. Eighty-four hours he was in the saddle. But the enemy cared little for all his prancing to and fro on blooded steed or raw colt. They ascended the river and entered Richmond, burned and destroyed to their hearts' content, reëmbarked and dropped down stream again. The militia were only beginning to assemble when the British were back entrenching themselves in Leslie's deserted camp. The Governor returned to the devastated village which constituted his capital. He had shown that he was deficient in prompt decision; in a word, that he was not the man for the place and the times.

The invaders seemed to be established for a long stay and with slight chance of being disturbed; for the "fatal want of arms" still continued. There was not a regular soldier in the State, nor arms to put in the hands of the militia. Matters were nearly as bad as in North Carolina where, Jefferson wrote, the Americans could be saved only by the "moderation and caution" of their adversaries— a slender dependence indeed! It added to the exasperation of the Virginians that the traitor, Arnold, was in command upon their soil. Jefferson tried to devise a scheme for kidnapping him; but it may be conceived that such a bird was not to be snared by such a fowler.

For several months the British kept Virginia in a state of nervous inquietude. It is easy to imagine how Jefferson, as the winter and spring crept forward on leaden heels, must have counted first the months, then the weeks, then even the very days, which had yet to elapse before his painful responsibility would reach its end. For the second year of his administration would close on June 1, and he had wisely resolved not to be a candidate for reëlection. Possibly mutterings of dissatisfaction alarmed him for his success. But in his autobiography he says: "From a belief that, under the pressure of the invasion under which we were then laboring, the public would have more confidence in a military chief; and that, the military commander being invested with the civil power also, both might be wielded with more energy, promptitude, and effect for the defence of the State, I resigned the administration at the end of my second year." There was some talk among the discouraged Virginians, during the dark days now close at hand, of setting over themselves a dictator. This classic but mistaken expedient Jefferson had the good sense to oppose; he afterward said that "the very thought alone was treason against the people, was treason against mankind in general." Fortunately, his remonstrances prevailed in due season.

April came and was fast passing. Only May remained before the wearied Governor would be governor no longer. But fortune had yet one more buffet to deal him at parting. In the latter part of April, Cornwallis set out on a northward march, and, laying waste as he advanced, came into Virginia; by May 20 he was in Petersburg. The State lay at his mercy. Jefferson could devise nothing better than to implore Washington to hasten to its rescue. The Legislature, which had thrice already since the year came in fled in alarm from Richmond, had been adjourned to meet on May 24 at the safer village of Charlottesville, at the foot of the hills on which was Monticello. It was not till May 28 that a quorum came together and then they deferred from day to day the election of a new governor. Jefferson's term expired, but still he had to hold over, since no successor had been chosen. Things were in this condition when, on June 4, the early summer sun not having yet risen, a hard-ridden steed was reined up at the Governor's door. The rider had galloped in the night from an eastward county-town to say that a small body of British cavalry under the dreaded Tarlton was pushing rapidly along the road to Charlottesville and Monticello; they would probably be hardly three hours behind him. In this emergency Jefferson certainly showed no lack of personal courage. That is to say, he was not panic-stricken. He did not go to Charlottesville, because he wisely reflected that the members of the Legislature were able to run away from the town without his assistance. He stayed tranquilly at home, breakfasted, sent away his family, and concealed his plate and papers, all very leisurely. Indeed, he owed his escape from capture more to good luck than to any intelligent precaution on his own part. Had he fallen into the enemy's hands he would have been thought to have acted stupidly. As it turned out he did get safely away into the woods, and Colonel Tarlton, disappointed of his prey, had only to ride back again. But the ignominious scattering of all the ruling officials of the State served to fasten still another irritating, though really undeserved, stigma upon Jefferson's administration. It was the more vexatious because he ought to have been freed several days before from so much as a technical responsibility. He was also then, and long afterward, made very angry by imputations upon his courage, as though his flight had been ignominious. It is needless to say that it was not so. He could hardly have been expected to stand alone in his doorway and shoot at the body of dragoons.

Tarlton's men appear to have taken nothing at Jefferson's house beyond food and drink, in which refreshment even the owner himself could hardly have wished to stint them in that land of unquestioning hospitality. Jefferson afterward said: "Tarlton behaved very genteelly with me." But at another of his farms, which fell within reach of Cornwallis' force, Jefferson fared worse. It was not long since certain British commissioners, nominally sent on a futile errand of reconciliation, had declared that the inevitable conclusion of events must be that the colonies would become dependents of the French crown, and that England designed to make the gain of as little value to France as possible. The innuendo of this announcement was soon made the basis of practical operations; and the British armies, devoting themselves more to devastation than to warfare, harried the country upon all sides. Jefferson suffered with the rest, and has left a formidable record of the pillage. All his husbanded crops and one hundred and fifty cattle, sheep, and hogs were seized for food; all his growing crops were wantonly destroyed, and all his fences were burned; not only were his many valuable horses taken, but the throats of colts too young to be used were barbarously cut. Thirty slaves also were carried away. "Had this been to give them freedom," Jefferson said, Cornwallis "would have done right; but it was to consign them to inevitable death from the small-pox and putrid fever then raging in his camps," as in fact became their wretched fate. It is not surprising that in later days Jefferson cherished a bitter hostility towards a nation which had not only curtailed his popularity and reputation among his countrymen, but had also attacked his property in a spirit of extermination.

The censorious temper which many Virginians felt towards Jefferson found open expression in the Legislature during the last few months of his administration; and even some preparation, though just how much cannot be accurately ascertained, was made for an investigation. Certain it is that Mr. George Nicholas moved for an inquiry at the next session,* and that he was by no means without supporters. The prevalence of this sort of talk cut Jefferson deeply and he went out of office in a very bitter frame of mind, resolved to leave forever the public service. He only wished to return to the next session of the Legislature in order to court the threatened inquiry. To enable him to do this a member resigned, and then Albemarle County paid him the handsome honor of electing him one of its delegates, actually by an unanimous vote. Having taken his seat, he stated to the House his wish to meet the charges lately made against him. No one replied. He then read certain "objections" which had been informally furnished to him by Nicholas, and gave his reply to them. Still no one rose to assail him. It was in December, 1781, and the recent surrender of Cornwallis at Yorktown had probably softened somewhat the recent asperities. His friends became sufficiently emboldened to offer a resolution, which was readily passed, thanking him for his "impartial, upright, and attentive" administration, bearing testimony to his "ability, rectitude, and integrity," and avowing a purpose thus to remove "all unmerited censure." The closing phrase might mean much or little, and the adjectives and nouns, shrewdly selected, did not express exhaustive praise of an administration in time of war. But the whole constituted a mollifying application and an agreement to have done with unkindly criticism. Washington also had closed with some courteous words a letter, which he had lately found occasion to write to Jefferson, making a sort of certificate of good character. With such comfort as he could find in these testimonials, Jefferson withdrew to private life. He had had the misfortune to be

---

*Jefferson afterward was on friendly terms with Nicholas, saying that he was an able and honest man, and that this motion was the blunder of an ardent youth. Nicholas also afterward made the *amende honorable* to Jefferson.

placed in a position for which he was ill adapted, and in which perhaps no one could have given satisfaction. He had merited some
praise and some censure, and got less of the former and more of the
latter than was quite just. Altogether he had had decidedly hard
fortune.

CHAPTER VI

IN CONGRESS AGAIN

THE EX-GOVERNOR HAD experienced a wound far too deep to be healed by the gentle palliative administered by the Legislature. In an extremely bitter and resentful frame of mind, he moodily secluded himself at home, and reiterated upon every opportunity his resolve never again to be drawn forth into public life. He busied himself with his plantations, the education of his children, and the care of his invalid wife. In the winter months, early in 1782, he put the finishing touches to a labor which he had begun in the preceding spring, his well-known and useful "Notes on Virginia." In the spring of the same year he obstinately refused to attend the session of the Legislature though he was still a member. His enemies severely criticised this conduct, which his friends could not easily defend: Madison privately deplored such a display of irreconcilable temper, and Monroe more openly wrote him a plain letter of rebuke. But he was not to be moved; his only reply was a reiteration of his rankling sense of injury and his obstinate purpose to have done forever with the public service.

Yet it is probable that a more amiable incentive for such conduct mingled with his anger, though he was too proud and too hurt to name it. For his wife was in very ill health. In May, 1782, she lay in with her sixth child, and thereafter there could be no real hope of her recovery. Jefferson was tender and assiduous in his care of her as it was possible for man to be, and when at last, in September, the final day came, the scene was a terrible one. For three weeks after she died he did not leave his room; afterward he had recourse to long wanderings in the solitary wood-paths of the mountain. His oldest daughter was his constant companion during these weeks of intense grief, of which she has left a harrowing picture, showing Jefferson to have been not only affectionate but very emotional in temperament.

It is said that Mrs. Jefferson, almost in the extreme moment, begged her husband never to give her children a stepmother, and the pledge which he then so solemnly made, he ever faithfully kept. Henceforth Martha, his firstborn child, was to hold the warmest corner in his heart. She and Mary, the fourth child, were the only ones of six that were born to him who lived to mature years, and only Martha survived him. But the children of his brother-in-law, Dabney Carr, who had died young and poor, had been taken into his home, and remained there like his own. He was not only very kind and fond towards all these young people of his household, but he gave to their bringing up a conscientious and untiring care.* The letters which he wrote to them, and which have been reproduced with encomiums by admiring biographers, are always absurdly didactic and often remind the reader of the effusions of the late Mrs. Barbauld, or of the virtue and wisdom enshrined in the pages of "Sanford and Merton;" but they are kindly and indicative of a lively interest.

In September, 1776, Congress nominated Jefferson, with Franklin and Deane, to frame a treaty of alliance and commerce with France; but he declined the mission. In June, 1781, he was

---

*The list of Jefferson's children is as follows:—Martha Jefferson, born September 27, 1772, married to Thomas Mann Randolph on February 23, 1790, died October 10, 1836; Jane Randolph Jefferson, born April 3, 1774, died September 1775; a son, born May 28, 1777, died June 14, 1777; Mary (or Maria) Jefferson, born August 1, 1778, Married to John W. Eppes on October 13, 1797, and died April 17, 1804; a daughter, born November 3, 1780, died April 15, 1781; Lucy Elizabeth Jefferson, born May 8, 1782, died —— 1784.

again deputed to go abroad, with Franklin, Adams, Jay, and Laurens, to negotiate a treaty of peace; but again he pleaded personal reasons as an excuse. Two months after the death of his wife news came to him at the seat of his friend Colonel Cary, at Ampthill, where he was nursing his own children and the young Carrs through the process of inoculation, that he had been again appointed upon the same duty. The proposition came opportunely, offering an activity and change of scene at once wholesome and agreeable. He accepted, and made ready for departure; but the presence of French cruisers off the coast delayed the sailing of vessels, and before he could get away news came showing that the negotiations were so far advanced that his presence would be substantially useless. So in February, 1783, he again returned home.

But another door for reëntrance into public life was forthwith opened. On June 6, 1783, he was chosen by the Virginia Legislature a member of Congress, whither he repaired in November following. That body had fallen into something very like contempt, and many gentlemen conceived that the honor, such as it was, of membership need not entail the trouble of attendance. So it happened that, though the treaty of peace was to be ratified before a certain near date, only seven States were represented, whereas the assent of nine was necessary. Some members proposed that the seven should ratify, upon the chance that Great Britain would never detect the insufficiency. But this dishonorable expedient was vigorously opposed by Jefferson and others. At last an urgent appeal brought in some of the delinquent members; and Jefferson had the pleasure of signing the treaty which established the Independence declared in his document seven years before. It fell to him, also, to play an important part in arranging the ceremonial of Washington's resignation.

The need of an executive power more permanent than this intermittent Congress led Jefferson to propose a "committee of the

States," to be composed of one member from each State and to remain in session during the recesses. The plan was adopted, but resulted in complete failure by reason of factions in the committee. He showed a sounder wisdom in his criticism of Morris' report on the national finances. That gentleman, by ingenious figuring, had devised a money unit which was a perfectly accurate common measure between the currencies of all the States. This was the $\frac{1}{1440}$ part of a dollar. Jefferson justly found fault with a system which would make all the little computations of daily life ridiculously vast and complex. For example, he said, the price of a loaf of bread, $\frac{1}{20}$ of a dollar, would be 72 units; of a pound of butter, $\frac{1}{5}$ of a dollar, 288 units; of a horse, worth $80, 115,200 units; while a national debt of $80,000,000 would be 115,200,000,000 units. To escape such palpable folly he suggested the dollar as the unit.

Jefferson further had the pleasure of tendering to Congress Virginia's deed, ceding her vast northwestern territory to be held as the common property of all the States. Directly afterward he was made one of the committee charged to prepare a plan for the government of this region. The report was doubtless composed by him, since the draft in the State Department is in his handwriting. It contains the substance of the famous Ordinance of the Northwestern Territory. Its most honorable provision is, "that after the year 1800 of the Christian era, there shall be neither slavery nor involuntary servitude in any of the said States, otherwise than in punishment of crimes," etc. Yet beside this humane and noble piece of statesmanship we have a glimpse of that absurd element in Jefferson's mind which his admirers sought to excuse by calling him a "philosopher." The matter is small to be sure, but suggestive. He proposed as names for the several subdivisions of this territory: Sylvania, Michigania, Cherronesus, Assenisippia, Metropotamia, Illinoia, Saratoga, Washington, Polypotamia, and Pelisipia. Fortunately these wondrous classic titles have not afflicted the children of our common schools. But much less happily the clause prohibiting slavery was lost, only six of the Northeastern and Middle States voting for it.

Such were the last legislative undertakings of Mr. Jefferson. On May 7, 1784, he left Congress.

CHAPTER VII

MINISTER TO FRANCE

SIMULTANEOUSLY WITH HIS retirement from Congress Jefferson was for the fourth time appointed to a foreign mission. His errand was to aid Dr. Franklin and John Adams in negotiating treaties of commerce. He sailed from Boston July 5, 1784, and arrived in Portsmouth July 30. He proceeded at once to Paris, and soon established himself there in a handsome house, which he afterward exchanged for one of considerable magnificence, and in all respects he made arrangements for living in very good style. His salary was nine thousand dollars a year, and with all the aid he could get from his private fortune he was hard pushed to meet his expenses. His daughter Martha he placed at the most fashionable and exclusive convent school in the country.

He soon found that he could do little for the United States beyond representing them creditably and serving as a respectable sample of the new trans-Atlantic people. Nor were his duties much changed when, in the following spring, the trio of diplomatists was broken up by the departure of Franklin for home and of John Adams for England, and by his own appointment as resident minister to France. The unpleasant truth was that the ancient monarchies of Europe knew little and cared less for the parvenu republics of a distant continent, and were indifferent concerning commercial treaties with a people whose commerce was an unknown and unvalued quantity. "Lady Rockminster has took us up," said the

Begum Clavering to Pendennis; and very much in the same way France had taken up the North American States. She vouched for their respectability, treated them publicly with pointed courtesy, and affably extended to their representatives the hospitalities of her court for holding diplomatic intercourse with other powers. But when these other powers, though civil enough, were wholly uninterested, France could not further help her protégés. Indeed, she herself disappointed expectation when it came to actual business. Jefferson, who had decided notions about the advantages of free trade, was untiring in his efforts to mitigate the severity of the French regulations, and his diplomatic correspondence with Vergennes and Montmorin fairly reeks with the flavors of whale oils, saltfish, and tobacco. Yet he was able to accomplish scarcely anything.

He had also to encounter the usual humiliations which beset all American envoys for many years by reason of the financial embarrassments of the States. He lived in a hive of creditors of his nation, who seemed resolved, if they could not extort from him payment of their demands, at least to have their money's worth in tormenting him. He was further much irritated at being compelled to aid in arranging, on behalf of his countrymen, that disgraceful tribute which powerful civilized nations were wont to pay to the corsair states of Northern Africa. He strenuously urged that war would be more effectual, more honorable, and in the end not more costly, and he proposed to form a league of commercial nations to sustain a combined naval armament sufficient to overawe those pirates in their own waters. But his spirited and sensible efforts did not meet with the success which they deserved.

In the early spring of 1786 another unpleasant task awaited him. He was obliged to spend a few weeks in London in the hope of aiding Mr. Adams in sundry commercial negotiations there pending. He was presented, he says, "as usual, to the King and Queen at their levees, and it was impossible for anything to be more ungracious than their notice of Mr. Adams and myself." Also the Marquis of Caermarthen, Minister of Foreign Affairs, was so vague and evasive as to confirm Mr. Jefferson in his belief of the English "aversion to have anything to do with us." Naturally he achieved nothing and went away in no pleasant frame of mind, carrying personal reminiscences chiefly of coldness and insolence. His contempt and hatred towards England, much intensified by this trip, and his belief in the bitter hostility of that country towards the States, hereafter find frequent and vigorous expression in his correspondence.

> That nation hate us, their ministers hate us, and their King more than all other men. . . . Our overtures of commercial arrangements have been treated with derision. . . . I think their hostility towards us is much more deeply rooted at present than during the war.

> In spite of treaties, England is still our enemy. Her hatred is deep-rooted and cordial, and nothing is wanting with her but the power to wipe us and the land we live in out of existence.

> [The English] do not conceive that any circumstance will arise which shall render it expedient for them to have any political connection with us. They think we shall be glad of their commerce on their own terms. There is no party in our favor here, either in power or out of power. Even the opposition concur with the ministry and the nation in this.

> I think the King, ministers, and nation are more bitterly hostile to us at present than at any period of the late war.

> The spirit of hostility to us has always existed in the mind of the King, but it has now extended itself through

the whole mass of the people and the majority in the public councils.

I had never concealed . . . that I considered the British as our natural enemies and as the only nation on earth who wished us ill from the bottom of their souls. And I am satisfied that, were our continent to be swallowed up by the ocean, Great Britain would be in a bonfire from one side to the other.

So excessive was his distrust that he even "thought the English capable of administering aid to the Algerines."

He was further profoundly incensed at the bad character which persistent abuse by the English press was fastening upon his country among Europeans. "There was," he says, "an enthusiasm towards us all over Europe at the moment of the peace. The torrent of lies published unremittingly in every day's London papers first made an impression and produced a coolness. The republication of these lies in most of the papers of Europe . . . carried them home to the belief of every mind." The wretched credit of the States abroad is, he says, "partly owing to their real deficiencies, and partly to the lies propagated by the London papers, which are probably paid for by the minister to reconcile the people to the loss of us. No paper, therefore, comes out without a dose of paragraphs against America."

This state of popular feeling in England filled Jefferson with forebodings for the future. "In a country where the voice of the people influences so much the measures of administration, and where it coincides with the private temper of the King, there is no pronouncing-on future events." "A like disposition [of hostility] on our part has been rising for some time. . . . Our countrymen are eager in their passions and enterprises and not disposed to calculate their interests against these." Reflecting that the animosities "which seize the whole body of a people, and of a people too who dictate their own measures, produce calamities of long duration," he said that he should "not wonder to see the scenes of ancient Rome and Carthage renewed in our days." But he consoled himself with the reflection that "we are young and can survive them; but their rotten machine must crush under the trial."

Jefferson was preëminently a man of peace; he instinctively loved it, and he knew that his own abilities fitted him only for peaceful scenes. About the time of which we are writing he remarked that "the most successful war seldom pays for its losses," and throughout life he hated everything which did not pay. He therefore deprecated a war even with England; yet he abominated her with that peculiar bitterness which is seldom cherished by more combative natures, but has a strange way of lurking in the obscure depths of pacific characters. Allowing for a little excess in this feeling, he was in the main perfectly right. It is necessary to dip very little beneath the tranquil surface of history to find a vast reservoir of evidence in corroboration of his views and justification of his feelings. He read English sentiments and purposes with perfect accuracy. But further, besides their enmity he plainly saw that perverse and obstinate dulness which was so long a marked trait in their intercourse with this country. With bitter justice he said, "our enemies (for such they are in fact) have for twelve years past followed but one uniform rule, that of doing exactly the contrary of what reason points out. Having early during our contest observed this in the British conduct, I governed myself by it in all prognostications of their measures; and I can say with truth it never failed me but in the circumstance of their making peace with us." He further ventured to say that the English "require to be kicked into common good manners." Yet he retained sufficient fairness to admit the excellence of the English system of government, reserving his condemnation chiefly for the behavior of the ministry and prominent men.

From this futile and exasperating English trip Jefferson returned to a thoroughly congenial society. If, as these Parisian years glided pleasantly by, they seemed fraught with little matter of importance for the States, and to be chiefly instrumental in promoting Jefferson's personal gratification, it was only because their true bearing was not yet apparent. It was seed-time, and the harvest was not to ripen until Jefferson should become the leader of a powerful party in the United States. Then English insolence and French courtesy began severally to bear their appropriate fruits, and the gathering was a matter of some consequence to all concerned.

Mr. Jefferson's stay in France extended through five years. When he arrived, the monarchy seemed firmly established as ever; before he left, the Bastille had been destroyed, blood had been freely spilled in the streets, mobs had overawed the king and slain cabinet ministers. No Frenchman watched events with more profound interest than did Jefferson, and none had better opportunities than he enjoyed for observing the gradual advance of revolutionary feeling. His own predilections and his natural intimacy with Lafayette brought him from the outset into the society of the liberal or patriotic party. These men, moderate and reasonable reformers and not at all identical with the violent revolutionists of later stages, found in him a kindred spirit, long accustomed to think the thoughts which they were just beginning to think, and to hold the beliefs which they were now acquiring. They made of him at once an instructor, counsellor, and sympathizing friend. They recognized him as one of themselves, a speculative thinker concerning the rights of mankind, a preacher of extreme doctrines of political freedom, a deviser of theories of government, a propounder of vague but imposing generalizations, a condemner of the fetters of practicability, in a word, in the slang of that day, a "philosopher;" and they liked him accordingly. Upon his own part, his interest in the reformation of their odious royal despotism could hardly have been greater, had he himself been a Frenchman. He went daily to Versailles to attend the debates of the National Assembly. Lafayette and others sought his suggestions. The Archbishop of Bordeaux, as head of a committee of the National Assembly, charged to draft the *projet* of a constitution, actually invited him "to attend and assist at their deliberations." This he wisely declined to do. But later, in private conference with one or two personal friends, he proposed an important step,—that "the King, in a *séance royale*, should come forward with a charter of rights in his hand, to be signed by himself and by every member" of the Assembly; and he actually sketched the chief heads of such a "charter."

If these acts seem an interference of questionable propriety, yet upon the whole it must be admitted that he behaved with excellent discretion and self-control, though the temptation to mingle in affairs was rendered exceptionally great by his real interest in them, by the abnormal state of political matters, by his friendship with Lafayette and others, and by the deference which was shown to him personally, indicative of the influence which he might exert. Only once did he appear in danger of being seriously compromised, and then it was through the blunder of another. Lafayette, without previously consulting him, arranged that six or eight discordant chiefs of different sections of the liberal party in the Assembly should dine at Jefferson's house, in the hope that they might reach an agreement. Jefferson was much annoyed at this "inadvertence" on the part of his friend, and waited on Count Montmorin the next morning with an explanation. The Count replied that

> he already knew everything which had passed, that so far from taking umbrage at the use made of my house on that occasion he earnestly wished I would habitually assist at such conferences, being sure I should be useful in moderating the warmer spirits and promoting a whole-

some and practicable reformation only. I told him I knew too well the duties I owed to the King, to the nation, and to my own country, to take any part in councils concerning their internal government, and that I should persevere with care in the character of a neutral and passive spectator, with wishes only and very sincere ones, that those measures might prevail which would be for the greatest good of the nation.

It has been the fashion to say that the feelings and ideas gathered by Jefferson in France constituted the predominant influence throughout his subsequent political career. In this there is much exaggeration, and towards him much injustice. His character was more independent. Moreover, he was a mature man when he went abroad, and had been busied from early youth, alike in the way of theory and practice, with the political and social problems of government. The originating disposition and radical temper of his mind had appeared from the outset, and were only confirmed, not created, by his foreign experience. Neither was his affection for France, nor his antipathy to England, then first implanted. Both sentiments were strong before he crossed the Atlantic; they were only encouraged by the pleasures of his long residence in the one country, and the convictions borne in upon him during his brief visit to the other. His character would be ill understood if it were supposed that his subsequent political career was the exotic growth of French seeds, instead of being developed in ordinary course from the native root. He would always have been a radical, an extreme democrat, a hater of England, a lover of France, a sympathizer with the French revolutionists, though he had never sailed out of sight of American shores. The only effect of his European life was to corroborate prëexisting opinions, and somewhat to intensify sentiments already entertained. Perhaps these were naturally so strong that a counteracting influence would have been more wholesome; and this might have been experienced had he remained to witness the Reign of Terror and the ascendancy of Robespierre. This, however, was not to be. In September, 1789, he sailed for home from Havre, upon what he supposed to be a short leave of absence granted at his urgent request. But events, as will be seen, rendered his stay at home permanent.

Jefferson ought to have been a happy man when he set sail on this return trip. Never did an involuntary exile glorify, in imagination, his lost home as Jefferson had been glorifying the States for five years past. All the charms of Paris were to him as nothing in comparison with the merits of his dear native land. "London," he said, "though handsomer than Paris, is not so handsome as Philadelphia!" In the way of education, only vice and modern languages were better taught in Europe than at home; instruction was just as good at William and Mary College as at the most famous seats of learning abroad! He begged Monroe to come to France, because "it will make you adore your own country, its soil, its climate, its equality, liberty, laws, people, and manners." He predicted that many Europeans would settle in America, but "no man now living will ever see an instance of an American removing to settle in Europe and continuing there." The virtues of his fellow-citizens he attributes to the fact that they have "been separated from their parent stock and kept from contamination, either from them or the other people of the old world, by the intervention of so wide an ocean." "With all the defects of our Constitution, . . . the comparison of our governments with those of Europe is like a comparison of heaven and hell. England, like the earth, may be allowed to take the intermediate station."

To the gaze of such a patriot everything which took place in his own country seemed admirable. Even Shays's insurrection in Massachusetts, which, by the alarm that it spread among all thinking men, contributed largely to the adoption of the new Constitution, seemed to Jefferson a commendable occurrence. Undeniably he talked some very bad nonsense about it.

> The commotions offer nothing threatening; they are a proof that the people have liberty enough, and I could not wish them less than they have. If the happiness of the mass of the people can be secured at the expense of a little tempest, now and then, or even of a little blood, it will be a precious purchase.

> To punish these errors too severely would be to suppress the only safeguard of the public liberty.

> A little rebellion now and then is a good thing, . . . an observation of this truth should render honest republican governors so mild in their punishment of rebellions as not to discourage them too much. It is a medicine necessary for the sound health of government.

> Thus I calculate,—an insurrection in one of thirteen States in the course of eleven years that they have subsisted, amounts to one in any particular State in one hundred and forty three years, say a century and a half. This would not be near as many as have happened in every other government that has ever existed. So that we shall have the difference between a light and a heavy government as clear gain.

> Can history produce an instance of rebellion so honorably conducted? . . . God forbid we should ever be twenty years without such a rebellion. . . . What signify a few lives lost in a century or two? The tree of liberty must be refreshed from time to time with the blood of patriots and tyrants. It is its natural manure.

It shakes one's faith in mankind to find a really great statesman uttering such folly! It had not even the poor excuse of being caught from the French revolutionists; for the latest of these sentences was uttered in November, 1787, when Jefferson was more probably engaged in imparting such extravagant notions to the moderate French reformers than in receiving these wild ideas from them. In truth, Jefferson was recoiling too far from the "conspiracy of kings and nobles," and was cast for a time into the ridiculous position of advocating a "no government" theory. "The basis of our governments," he said, "being the opinion of the people, the very first object should be to keep that right,"—a sound postulate which he makes the pedestal for a preposterous superstructure; for he adds, "were it left to me to decide whether we should have a government without newspapers, or newspapers without a government, I should not hesitate a moment to prefer the latter,"—the newspapers of the latter half of the eighteenth century! "I am convinced," he says, "that those societies (as the Indians) which live without government enjoy in their general mass an infinitely greater degree of happiness than those who live under the European governments. Among the former public opinion is in the place of law, and restraining morals as powerfully as laws ever did anywhere." "Societies exist under three forms; . . . 1. Without government as among our Indians. 2. Under governments wherein the will of every one has a just influence. . . . 3. Under governments of force. . . . It is a problem not clear in my mind that the first condition is not the best." One loses patience with an intelligent man talking such stuff.

Jefferson's experience abroad, in attempting to form commercial treaties, had taught him the necessity of a closer union of the States for purposes of foreign relationships; but when the lesson of Shays's insurrection was even read backwards by him, it is easy to see that he was far from comprehending the domestic necessity for a much firmer consolidation. "My general plan," he said, "would be to make the States one as to everything connected with foreign nations, and several as to everything purely domestic." Such being his opinion, it was inevitable that when the Constitution of the United States was published, he found much in it which seemed to him very unsound and objectionable. There are in the document, he said, "things which stagger all my dispositions to subscribe to what such an assembly has proposed," and his earliest criticisms were very severe. Further consideration, however, the arguments of the Federalist, and correspondence with Madison and Monroe, gradually induced him to modify his views. By May, 1788, he was able to say: "I look forward to the general adoption of the new Constitution with anxiety, as necessary for us under our present circumstances." If in many particulars he was still imperfectly pleased, he was only of the like sentiment with most of the zealous advocates of adoption. Probably every prominent man among the Federalists could, in his own opinion, have suggested improvements. Jefferson finally took the national charter as its other supporters did, "contented with the ground which it will gain for us, and hoping that a favorable moment will come for correcting what is amiss in it." His earlier wish was that nine States would adopt it, "in order to insure what was good in it, and that the others might, by holding off, produce the necessary amendments." But later he declared the plan of Massachusetts to be "far preferable," and expressed the hope that it would "be followed by those who are yet to decide." Finally on December 4, 1788, he writes, "I have seen with infinite pleasure our new Constitution accepted by eleven States, not rejected by the twelfth; and that the thirteenth happens to be a State of the least importance."

The preceding extracts, which might be multiplied by many more of identical tenor, abundantly show Jefferson's real sentiments concerning the Constitution, and refute the unfair charge afterward brought against him by his enemies, that he was opposed to it. His own characteristic statement was, "I am not a Federalist, because I never submitted the whole system of my opinions to the creed of any party of men whatever, in religion, in philosophy, in politics, or in anything else where I was capable of thinking for myself. Such an addiction is the last degradation of a free and moral agent. If I could not go to heaven but with a party, I would not go there at all. Therefore I am not of the party of the Federalists. But I am much farther from that of the anti-Federalists. I approved, from the first moment, of the great mass of what is in the new Constitution." He then continues at great length to show how his objections gradually gave way before argument, until a confession of faith, too rigid to have been repeated by him, could have been repeated by very few individuals in the States. It is probable that the Constitution was nearer to his ideal upon the one side than it was to Hamilton's ideal upon the other. The only serious objections, which he retained to the end, were the absence of a bill of rights and the reëligibility of the President. The former real defect was promptly and wisely cured; the latter has been practically controlled by a wise custom which he himself helped to inaugurate.

CHAPTER VIII

SECRETARY OF STATE—DOMESTIC AFFAIRS

ON OCTOBER 23, 1789, Mr. Jefferson sailed from Cowes, and on December 23 he was welcomed by his slaves at Monticello. At his departure he had supposed that he was returning home for a visit of a few months only, and that he should speedily go back to watch the progress of the French Revolution. He was now so much more interested in this movement than in any other matter, that he was by no means gratified to find awaiting him, upon his arrival, an invitation from President Washington to fill the place of secretary of state. He replied that he did not prefer the change, but that he would be governed by the President's wishes. Washington thereupon wrote again in very urgent fashion, and Madison made a visit to Monticello for the express purpose of exerting his personal influence. Beneath such pressure Jefferson reluctantly abandoned his hope of remaining abroad, and accepted the secretaryship, only stipulating for a few weeks for setting in order his private affairs. It was not until March 21, 1790, that he arrived in New York and entered upon the duties of his office.

In those days the cabinet consisted of only four persons. John Jay had been acting temporarily as secretary of state, but with the understanding that he should be made chief justice so soon as a permanent secretary could be appointed; Hamilton had been made secretary of the treasury immediately after Washington's inauguration; about the same time Knox had been appointed secretary of war, and later Edmund Randolph had been made attorney-general. The great brunt of the labor in the organization of public affairs had fallen and still rested upon Hamilton, who had encountered the vast and complex task with magnificent spirit and ability. By the time that Jefferson came to share in the business of government, all questions concerning the foreign debt and the domestic national debt had been disposed of by Congress in accordance with Hamilton's recommendations. But there still remained, as a bone of fierce contention, the secretary's scheme for the assumption by the United States of the war debts of the individual States; and concerning this the opposing parties had been wrought up to a pitch of exceeding bitterness and excitement. In committee of the whole in the House of Representatives the assumption had been carried by thirty-one yeas to twenty-six nays; but when the question came to be taken in the House proper the representatives from North Carolina had arrived, and aided in turning the scale, so that on March 29 the measure was voted down. From the condition of feeling it was evident that a serious crisis already menaced the young nation. Congress met daily and adjourned without transacting any business; the hostile factions could not work together upon any subject, and, indeed, nobody cared to think or talk of anything save assumption. Threats of disunion were heard on all sides. Hamilton contemplated the emergency with profound anxiety, for the Treasury Department carried within itself the fate of the new government; and upon his financiering really depended the existence of a people. The momentous struggle called forth all the resources of his ingenious and fertile mind. While he kept up a steady fight all along the front, he also set himself to devise a flank movement, and in this manœuvre he resolved to make use of Mr. Jefferson.

It happened opportunely that the selection of a site for the national capital had given rise to an eager sectional division in Congress. The Southern States wanted it on the Potomac; the Middle and Eastern States wished it to be farther north. The north-

ern party had prevailed by a narrow majority. Now it was fortunately the case that the parties in the assumption debate had
divided by the like sectional lines; the Middle and Eastern States
were in favor of assumption; the Southern States were opposed to
it; and in this matter the South had prevailed, also by a slender
majority. The opportunity for a bargain was obvious; the temptation to it was irresistible; the justification was sufficiently satisfactory. Hamilton accordingly resolved to buy two or three votes for
his assumption scheme at the price of the required number of votes
for the Potomac site. In this bit of political commerce he selected
Jefferson as an efficient partner. So one day, meeting Jefferson in
the street, Hamilton walked with him and discussed the matter. He
depicted the national jeopardy in woful colors, and movingly
besought Jefferson to use his influence with some of his friends
and to save the Union. Jefferson replied that he was "really a
stranger to the whole subject," but that the preservation of the
country touched him nearly, and he begged Hamilton to dine with
him the next day, to meet one or two more whom he would invite,
in the hope that together they might devise some acceptable "compromise." The dinner came off, Jefferson afterward wrote that he
himself "could take no part in [the discussion] but an exhortatory
one," because he was a "stranger to the circumstances which
should govern it." But the bargain was then and there struck; and
at that dinner-table assumption was bought for a capital on the
Potomac. The terms of the agreement were punctually fulfilled.
The requisite number of votes were delivered, so to speak, on both
sides, and Hamilton's financial policy prevailed without mutilation.

Soon, however, Jefferson found himself deeply repenting his
share in this transaction. He began to doubt whether the measure
was really wise and right, and he plainly saw that from a personal
and selfish point of view he had blundered seriously. For he had
greatly aided the prestige and influence of one who soon became
his most formidable political opponent, and he had been largely

efficient in achieving the success of a measure which his party was forthwith to single out for especial denunciation. When, therefore, he was pushed ere long to find explanations of this compromising fellowship with Hamilton, he behaved like the fog who gnaws off his own leg to escape from the trap; he sacrificed, by denial, one of the most marked of his mental traits, his political astuteness; he said that he had been tricked by Hamilton, and made a dupe and tool in a department of business with which he was unfamiliar, that he had been "most ignorantly and innocently made to hold the candle" for the wicked game of the Secretary of the Treasury. Such a defence seemed a bad advertisement of his fitness for political leadership, and was otherwise so poor and incredible that it would not have been resorted to, could any other have been devised. The bargain which had been made was perfectly plain and simple, at least in respect of political morality, and so far as this went could be explained and comprehended in five minutes. As for the soundness of the policy of assumption, Jefferson could have heard little else talked about since his arrival at New York. He knew the bitterness of the contest concerning it, and if he had not made up his mind about it, he was rash in taking sides so decisively. But if he had been rash he was not therefore entitled to abuse Hamilton for setting forth and promoting his own views.* The truth is not, however, buried out of sight beneath his excuses and explanation of his action. This truth is, that he was asked and that he consented to take a part before he comprehended or even suspected the powerful formative energies which ran under the surface of Hamilton's financial measures, like sinews beneath the skin. He was, therefore, willing enough to help forward a measure upon which seemed to depend the continuance of the Union, and of which the remoter bearing and effects lay beyond his vision. A little later he appreci-

---

*As evidence that Jefferson understood very well what he was about, and had his own wishes in the matter, see his letter to Monroe of June 20, 1790, and letter to Gilmer of June 27, 1790.

ated that Hamilton had not only been handling the finances with singular technical skill, but had also been so shaping all his measures that they had constituted so many tonic doses administered to the national government, strengthening it, confirming it in the interests of an influential portion of the community, and exercising a powerful centralizing influence. When all this dawned upon Jefferson's understanding, he was filled with horror and indignation at the share he had unwittingly taken in promoting principles of government which he abominated. Also he was seriously irritated at the inconvenient light in which he had thus been made to appear before those with whom he sought political fellowship and authority. Then, his eyes being at last opened, anger against Hamilton induced him to assert that Hamilton had outwitted him by taking unfair advantage of his inexperience.

Jefferson was no financier. The shrewd good sense which he had displayed in managing his own business, as a planter, was superseded by an uncontrollable passion for theorizing, when he came to grapple with the great and intricate problems of national finances. At times he wandered into the wildest and most absurd vagaries. Thus, only a few months before he took his seat in the cabinet, he had been much pleased with a novel idea that had struck him concerning "a question of such consequences as not only to merit decision, but place also among the fundamental principles of every government." It is with some astonishment that the patient reader follows through several pages of guileless argument the development of this grand, fundamental, newly-discovered truth, and finally learns the confounding doctrine that no public debt can rightfully survive the generation which contracts it! The daring and original logician starts with the "self-evident" proposition that "the earth belongs in usufruct to the living; that the dead have neither powers nor rights over it." But, he says, if a debt survives the generation which contracts it, then the subsequent generation takes "the earth" subject to a burden imposed by and for the dead. This must needs be wrong, since it is counter to a "self-evident" premise. Now assuming that men come of age at twenty-one, and that the majority of those who are alive at twenty-one will live thirty-four years more, it follows that a generation may contract debts to run thirty-four years and no longer. This period he afterward reduced to nineteen years; for "a generation consisting of all ages, and which legislates by all its members above the age of twenty-one years, cannot contract for so long a time, because their majority will be dead much sooner." It is at once ludicrous, pitiful, and alarming to hear such rubbish from an influential leader of the people. After listening to it one is not surprised to bear that in criticising the work of one of the greatest financiers whom the world has ever seen, Jefferson made but a sorry show.

Nevertheless, being profoundly unconscious of his own incapacity in this department of knowledge, Jefferson did not refrain from free indulgence in such dangerous criticism. He was wont to say that Hamilton's financial system was designed to serve as a puzzle for excluding popular understanding and inquiry. In 1802 he wrote to Gallatin concerning Hamilton:—

> In order that he might have the entire government of his machine, he determined so to complicate it as that neither the President nor Congress should be able to understand it or to control him. He succeeded in doing this, not only beyond their reach, but so that he himself could not unravel it. He gave to the debt in the first instance, in funding it, the most artificial and mysterious form he could devise. He then moulded up his appropriations of a number of scraps and remnants, many of which were nothing at all, and applied them to different objects in reversion and remainder, until the whole system was involved in impenetrable fog.

He actually reiterated this declaration so late as 1818, long after the perfect practical success of that renowned system had constituted its unanswerable vindication. But it is not probable that he was disingenuous in his abuse, for certainly Hamilton's financiering was from the beginning, and ever remained, a "puzzle" utterly insoluble for Mr. Jefferson. Nevertheless he persisted in a blind hatred and denunciation, eloquent enough while he confined himself to generalities, but, so often as he turned to more specific fault-finding, manifesting a surprising ignorance of economic principles and a hopeless confusion of thought. Yet a distinguished feature of Hamilton's system was its grand, plain simplicity, not only in its broad outlines, but in matters of detail and technique. His reports to Congress were lucid to a degree which makes them comprehensible to a woman or a child. It befell, however, very fortunately for Jefferson, that he had not much fighting to do in a field in which he was so little at home. By the time that the antagonism between him and Hamilton had become fairly developed, all the principal features of Hamilton's financial scheme, except only the national bank, had become complete and adopted parts of the governmental machinery. There was no need, therefore, to encounter them with argument, but only to revile them in a broad way.

It has been said that Washington formed his cabinet with a deliberate purpose of amalgamating parties by bringing together, as political comrades, the two chief representatives of opposing opinions. This erroneous statement has been sustained by two other incorrect propositions, namely, (1) that Jefferson was opposed to the Constitution which Hamilton befriended, a theory already shown to be untrue; (2) that he and Hamilton had respectively from the beginning established policies antagonistic to each other, which is a palpable misrepresentation. For a while all was doubtful and tentative concerning both men and measures in the new government, although the outcome now appears to have been so strictly in accordance with the logic of circumstances, and the native bent and qualities of the different individuals, that it is difficult not to carry back the later opinions and knowledge to a date at which neither could have existed. It took some time for this logic and these qualities to become apparent to the chief actors, who learned each other's ways of thinking only by degrees. Meanwhile Hamilton and Jefferson met upon a friendly footing, and for a time apparently entertained no suspicion that they would not be able to pursue an harmonious policy. Indeed, there hardly were at first two parties or two systems of national politics in the country. The material for forming these lay ready at hand in the natural constitution of men's minds, but it still reposed like ore in the mine, half unseen and wholly unshaped. There were those who always instinctively said Nay to all proposals coming from Hamilton; but they were not an organized party, and had no defined policy of their own. It was very gradually that what deserved to be called a hostile school of political thought was developed by the measures of the government. Only as the Hamiltonian structure grew piece by piece did the design of the builder appear to be much more comprehensive than had been at first understood. Then it was seen that Hamilton, besides substituting order for confusion, and solvency for insolvency, had also been creating a very powerful governmental machine; then men saw how deep down in the nation he had succeeded in setting the foundations of the government, and what extensive powers he had grasped for it, by construing the Constitution to his purpose. They remembered that he theoretically believed in a monarchical form, and they saw that he was fast making this republican government not less strong and centralized than a limited monarchy. Then the men of democratic minds became combined together through their common alarm; and as no man was more thoroughly democratic than Jefferson, so no man was more profoundly alarmed. We have but to recall his talk about the charms of newspapers without a government, and about the excellence of the Indian form of polity, to conceive the horror with which he beheld this rapid transformation of a federal league into a national unit. No sooner did he get a notion of the ruinous course by which Hamilton was steering the ship, than he began to whisper warnings among the passengers, to organize a species of mutiny against one who, in truth, had no more exclusive right to the helm than he himself had. So the period of confidence between Hamilton and Jefferson endured only for a limited time, and though they remained personal friends for a short while after they had become political opponents, yet such accusations and personalities as were soon cast against each by the friends and followers of the other ere long destroyed all traces of good feeling, and they distrusted and hated each other, and fought and denounced each other bitterly, and believed every possible ill of each other during the rest of their lives.

Most unfortunately for his own good fame, Jefferson allowed himself to be drawn by this feud into the preparation of the famous "Anas." His friends have hardly dared to undertake a defence of those terrible records, and the very manner of those apologies which some have ventured to present has been fatal to their efficacy. The editor of the Congressional edition of Jefferson's works excuses the insertion of these post-mortuary slanders on the ground of editorial duty, and only reluctantly suffers himself to become the formal agent of their perpetuation. But there is no symptom that Jefferson thought that it was unbecoming in him to set down all the idle rumors, the slander and gossip received at third and fourth hand, the malicious tales of enemies, aimed at the good fame of an adversary who, at least, had never dealt him an unfair blow, and to leave this odious collection of poisonous scraps to be published not only after the death of that adversary, and so late that no substantial opportunity of contradictions by contemporary evidence remained, but also after his own death, so that he could not be called upon to sustain his statements, or punished for failure to do so. It must be confessed that the compilation of these

unfortunate and most disreputable fragments is among the mean-
est acts recorded by history, and that it has more impaired
Jefferson's good name than all the other mistakes of his life and all
the assaults of his enemies. Had he been able to resist the temptation to seek such an ignoble revenge on a dead foe, he would have
lived in history as a man of a far more honorable spirit than can now
be attributed to him.

CHAPTER IX

SECRETARY OF STATE—GROWTH OF DISSENSIONS

JEFFERSON WAS THE most astute and successful politician who has yet flourished in a country singularly and unfortunately prolific of this not very estimable race. But he was very much more than a politician, and he added something even to the essential traits of a statesman; he was a profound thinker concerning the theory of government and the principles of social and political organization. In full accord with the new spirit of his era, he was a radical even among radicals, and a democrat of the extreme class. He could hardly bring himself to declare that the people should govern, because he had a lurking notion that there should be no government at all. "The rights of man," the favorite slang phrase of the day, signified to his mind an almost entire absence of governmental control. His milder opponents called him a visionary, and the hopeless impracticability of many of his theories almost justified the term. His more bitter assailants stigmatized him as dishonest; and there certainly was an element of disingenuousness in his character, a covert habit in his dealings, and a carelessness concerning the truth in small matters. But his belief in the doctrines of human freedom was a pure and deep conviction, an ineradicable portion of his nature. His faith in the laxest form of democracy, scarcely removed from anarchy, stood to him in the place of a religion; he preached it with a fervor, intensity, and constancy worthy of Mahomet or Wesley. It was an inevitable consequence of this vehement conviction that he regarded supporters of contrary principles with distrust and abhorrence as wicked men, conscious promulgators of falsehood in the most important of all human concerns. Evil reports concerning them seemed so intrinsically probable as always to command his ready belief; and there is no evidence that he ever refused to credit any malicious tale repeated against them, no matter how tainted in its origin or progress. He was observant and quick-witted, and soon appreciated the skill with which Hamilton was rapidly constructing a powerful centralized government. At Hamilton's back he beheld a disciplined body of able and ambitious men, some filling places of public trust and power, others absorbing wealth, all in one shape or another acquiring an extensive and irresistible influence in the body politic and social. Jefferson gazed upon this portentous growth with dread and repulsion. He saw enough to induce him fearfully to anticipate the destruction of human freedom in the United States, and he suspected much more than he saw. As he peered into the mystery of the Federalist policy, the vision of monarchy took shape before his eyes and long remained with him, an ever present and vivid terror. Henceforth in every measure of the Secretary of the Treasury he discerned an artful move in the monarchical game; at every social gathering of Federalists he seemed to hear the whispered plots of "Monocrats." If gentlemen, flushed with wine after dinner, made statements far outrunning their sober beliefs, their extravagant words were borne in exaggerated form to Jefferson's ears, were magnified by his excited mind, and were stored away by him as conclusive evidence of monarchical projects. The idea became a monomania with him. He wrote it to his friends, he jotted it down on the scraps of paper which afterward were gathered together for the "Anas;" he mournfully bore the gossip to Washington, and was not to be deterred from repeating it, though the President told him that he was talking nonsense.

Long afterward, looking back upon this period, Jefferson

declared that these dreadful monarchical tendencies had been visible to him from the earliest days of his arrival in New York.

> The President received me cordially, and my colleagues and the whole circle of principal citizens apparently with welcome. The courtesies of both political parties, given me as a stranger newly arrived among them, placed me at once in their familiar society. But I cannot describe the wonder and mortification with which the table conversations filled me. Politics were the chief topic, and a preference of kingly over republican government was evidently the favorite sentiment. An apostate I could not be, nor yet a hypocrite; and I found myself, for the most part, the only advocate on the republican side of the question, unless among the guests there chanced to be some member of that party from the legislative houses.

These sentences linger in that debatable land, somewhere in which exaggeration passes into falsehood. Evidently, in looking back down the long vista of nearly thirty years, Jefferson's vision was indistinct. If he had really been plunged into such a chilling bath of monarchy at once upon his arrival in New York, he would have cried out promptly at the sudden shock, and left contemporaneous evidence of it; whereas, in fact, some time elapsed before he began to give perceptible symptoms of distress at the unsound political faith about him. Monarchy was doubtless spoken of in a manner offensive to his democratic ears. The Constitution was a compromise wholly satisfactory to no one; the government was undeniably an experiment; and its probable efficiency was often discussed as an open question. Sentiments of loyalty, pride, and affection had not had time to strike deep root. But Jefferson made a mistake in construing an anxious doubt as equivalent to active disaffection; and was guilty of a gross, though certainly an unintentional, injustice in charging the advocates of a strong system with a design of changing the form of government. He was driven beyond his reason by foolish terrors when he spoke of Hamilton as the enemy of the Constitution. Every one has long since agreed that the Constitution had no other friend nearly so efficient as Hamilton. No man living had better means of knowledge concerning these matters than Washington, and no man was intellectually more capable of forming a correct judgment. Yet even Jefferson could not in his "Anas" set down the language, which the President held to him, in shape more corroborative of his views than this: "That with respect to the existing causes of uneasiness, he [Washington] thought there were suspicions against a particular party which had been carried a great deal too far. There might be desires, but he did not believe there were designs, to change the form of government into a monarchy; that there might be a few who wished it in the higher walks of life, particularly in the great cities, but that the main body of the people in the Eastern States were as steadily for republicanism as in the Southern." Making ever so slight allowance for refraction by reason of the transmission of these words through the Jeffersonian medium, we see the most inadequate basis for the vast pile of Jefferson's suspicion.

But in dealing with Jefferson's conduct, it is not the truth which must be sought so much as Jefferson's idea of the truth. That he had an honest belief in the monarchical conspiracy, and in the treasonable designs of the Hamiltonian clique, appears certain. Indeed, if he began with a faith like a grain of mustard seed, he must soon have caused it to expand into a vigorous tree, so liberally did he water it with the ceaseless iteration and reiteration of his own assertions. Frequent repetition of a statement assumes in time the aspect of evidence; and what he said so often he probably at last came to believe. Unquestionably he induced others to believe it. For years his talk was of "monarchists" and "monocrats," till the reader of his letters and memoirs regards these people like the sea-serpent, feels that it would be incongruous if so familiar a name did not represent some real existence, and in a way permits the fiction to be asserted into a reality. There was an earnestness, or, as he himself would have said, a venom, in Jefferson's language, when he dealt with this topic, indicating a force and depth of feeling hardly to be adequately conveyed by description, and which is so utterly inappropriate for a fable that it seems sufficiently to imply truth.

If the purpose of the monarchical party was abhorrent to Jefferson, so their means appeared consonantly base. The decision to pay in full not only the principal of the domestic debt, but also the arrears of interest, followed by the assumption of the State indebtedness, furnished, during a year and a half, opportunities for speculation which were availed of with an ardor that has not been surpassed in Wall Street in our own generation. Naturally those who gathered in the securities at low prices were the men of capital, sagacity, and enterprise, who lived in cities, more especially residents in New York and Philadelphia, who could best forecast congressional action. Naturally, too, those who had most faith in Hamilton plunged most boldly into the venture. Jefferson, therefore, and others who had taken fright at the monarchical scarecrow, were scandalized and alarmed as they saw the supporters of Hamiltonian measures reaping a great harvest of wealth, and consequently of political power and social consideration. They began to charge the Secretary of the Treasury with winning adherents by giving opportunities of growing suddenly and enormously rich. That great financial system which, in a few brief months, had raised the United States from a condition of pitiful and ignoble bankruptcy to the status of a solvent power in excellent credit, wore, to Jefferson's suspicious eyes, the aspect of a great, complex, and terribly efficient machine for building up in the State the most dangerous kind of aristocratical party.

His dissatisfaction was further nourished by other measures; the military establishment disgusted him, because he abhorred every manifestation of governmental power or control. The excise seemed odious, because he thought that all branches of internal taxation ought to be left to the States. But most of all the proposition for a national bank appeared to bristle with objectionable traits. By the time that Hamilton was prepared to push this project, the political operation of his financial policy was fully appreciated and, indeed, greatly exaggerated by Jefferson; nor was it longer possible for the treasury party to coerce support by declaring the existence of the Union to be at stake. This bank act involved first a question of law and then one of expediency. In the former aspect it presented much difficulty, and Washington asked for written opinions from his cabinet officers. Hamilton supported it in an argument which is one of the most famous of our state papers. Jefferson took the other side and argued the legal point, which alone he understood, with much force and ability. After great hesitation Washington decided to sign the bill. He was always reluctant to interfere with his secretaries in their respective departments; furthermore, if he was making a constitutional error it could be corrected by the Supreme Court. In due time that tribunal sustained the constitutionality of the bank, Chief Justice Marshall delivering an opinion in which he added nothing to the reasoning of Hamilton. But though the views of Jefferson were thus finally rejected, it must be acknowledged that the question, regarded as one purely of law, might just as well or better have been determined the other way. The issue was, whether a rigid or a liberal construction should be given to the general clauses of the Constitution; and a bench of strict constructionists would have encountered no insuperable legal obstacles in the way of sustaining Jefferson.

But if the legal and constitutional aspects and the political bearing of this measure were easily within Jefferson's comprehension, its relations to the finances and business of the country were far beyond his understanding. He proclaimed the most ignorant theories and talked the most absurd twaddle about its mischievous introduction of paper money, and the consequent banishment of gold and silver from circulation. When the subscription books were opened, he saw with melancholy forebodings the capitalists rushing forward in such eager competition that much more than the capital stock was quickly subscribed. He wrote gloomily to Monroe: "Thus it is that we shall be paying thirteen per cent. per annum for eight millions of paper money, instead of having that circulation of gold and silver for nothing. . . . For the paper emitted from the bank, seven per cent. profits will be received by the subscribers for it as bank paper, . . . and six per cent. in the public paper of which it is the representative. Nor is there any reason to believe that either the six millions of paper or the two millions of specie deposited will not be suffered to be withdrawn, and the paper thrown into circulation. The cash deposited by strangers for safe-keeping will probably suffice for cash demands." He was probably ignorant that such special deposits could not lawfully be used by the bank at all; and this is only a sample of his general lack of knowledge in all matters of business.

There is no doubt that the bank, whether constitutional or not, was of immense advantage to the country; but Jefferson could see in it only a prolific machine for turning out more corrupt supporters of that dangerous and designing monarchist, the Secretary of the Treasury. Henceforth his abuse of the "treasury party," as he called it, redoubled; nor did he ever modify this opinion to the end of his life. In his introduction to the "Anas," in 1818, he recorded that "Hamilton was not only a monarchist, but for a monarchy bottomed on corruption;" and he said that the bank was designed as an "engine of influence more permanent," for corrupting the Legislature, than the funding system and assumption could be. Accordingly "members of both houses," he said, "were constantly kept as directors who, on every question interesting to that institution or to the views of the Federal head, voted at the will of that head; and, together with the stockholding members, could always make the Federal vote that of the majority." On March 3, 1793, discussing Giles' famous resolutions of censure on Hamilton, he notes "the composition of the House, 1, of bank directors; 2, holders of bank stock; 3, stock jobbers; 4, blind devotees; 5, ignorant persons who did not comprehend them; 6, lazy and good humored persons, who comprehended and acknowledged them, yet were too lazy to examine, or unwilling to pronounce censure; the persons who knew these characters foresaw that, the three first descriptions making one third of the House, the three latter would make one half of the residue." It was thus that he endeavored to account for the ignominious failure of the anti-Federalist attempt to establish definite charges of dishonesty against Hamilton; and admitted his sympathy with the blunder of that unfortunate and disastrous measure.

Another thing which Jefferson beheld with horror was the national debt. Besides the speculation which soon ended in widespread ruin, he conceived that he detected a purpose on Hamilton's part to use this debt permanently, in some ingenious and covert way, as a perpetual resource for corrupting the Legislature. The fact that a portion of it had been made "deferred" for a few years, convinced him that Hamilton intended never to let the people pay what they owed and get clear of obligation. Everybody, he said, stood in dread of the "chickens of the treasury" and their "many contrivances." "As the doctrine is that a public debt is a public blessing, so they think a perpetual one is a perpetual blessing, and therefore wish to make it so large that we can never pay it off." He could not be induced to renounce this suspicion, even when a scheme was brought forward by Hamilton to promote payment within a short period. No evidence ever could persuade him that Hamilton was politically honest, and no lapse of time could allay his prejudices.

Washington, meanwhile, watched with profound concern the

schemes. In June, 1798, he wrote: —

> If on a temporary superiority of one of the parties the other
> is to resort to a scission of the union, no federal govern-
> ment can ever exist. If to rid ourselves of the present rule
> of Massachusetts and Connecticut, we break the Union,
> will the evil stop there? Suppose the New England States
> alone cut off, will our nature be changed? Are we not men
> still to the south of that, and with all the passions of men?
> Immediately we shall see a Pennsylvania and a Virginia
> party arise in the residuary confederacy, and the public
> mind will be distracted with the same party spirit. What a
> game, too, will the one party have in their hands by eter-
> nally threatening the other that unless they do so and so
> they will immediately join their northern neighbors. If we
> reduce our Union to Virginia and North Carolina, immedi-
> ately the conflict will be established between the repre-
> sentatives of these two States, and they will end by
> breaking into their simple units.

In other words, secession was a medicine which only one physi-
cian could be allowed to prescribe.

In March, 1800, both parties were already eagerly forecasting
the chances of the autumnal elections. Jefferson wrote: "The
Federalists begin to be very seriously alarmed about their election
next fall. Their speeches in private, as well as their public and private demeanor to me, indicate it strongly." After a careful discussion of the chances in the doubtful States, he cautiously declared
his own conclusion: "Upon the whole I consider it as rather more
doubtful than the last election, in which I was not deceived in more
than a vote or two;" but he allows it to be plainly read between the
lines that, though stopping short of actually predicting a
Republican success, he is really very sanguine of it. He had abundant ground for stronger hopes than he expressed.

The Federalists threw aside all scruples in conducting their campaign. A sample of the abuse and falsehood in which they dealt may be seen in one of the stories which they circulated concerning Jefferson, charging that "he had obtained his property by fraud and robbery; that in one instance he had defrauded and robbed a widow and fatherless children of an estate to which he was executor, of ten thousand pounds sterling, by keeping the property and paying them in money at the nominal rate, when it was worth no more than forty to one." The facts were stated by Jefferson to one of his friends as follows:

> I never was executor but in two instances, both of which having taken place about the beginning of the Revolution, which withdrew me immediately from all private pursuits, I never meddled in either executorship. In one of the cases only were there a widow and children. She was my sister. She retained and managed the estate in her own hands, and no part of it was ever in mine. In the other I was a copartner and only received on a division the equal portion allotted me. . . . Again, my property is all patrimonial, except about seven or eight hundred pounds' worth of lands, purchased by myself and paid for, not to widows and orphans, but to the very gentleman from whom I purchased.

These denials, he said, he would vouchsafe to his friend, but added, "I only pray that my letter may not go out of your hands, lest it should get into the newspapers, a bear-garden scene into which I have made it a point to enter on no provocation." He was probably the better able to keep this wise resolution, because he shrewdly appreciated that the rancor and personal malignity of his opponents were a sure indication of their sense of weakness and of coming defeat. The party which indulges most freely in false personal vituperation almost invariably finds itself beaten at the polls.

This result grew steadily more certain as the election drew nearer. The Federalists were disheartened and fore-doomed by the internal dissensions which split their party into factions more hostile and jealous towards each other than towards the common foe. The schism which Adams had opened could not be closed, and inevitable destruction awaited a house so divided against itself. Defeat was further insured by the admirable condition of the Republican party. It seems probable that for some time before the autumn of 1800, a fair polling of the people would have shown many more voters of Republican than of Federalist proclivities. It had been the ability and individual force of the Federalist leaders which had enabled them to maintain the party supremacy so long. But at last the Republicans had become thoroughly consolidated, and now, cheered by the spectacle presented by their discordant adversaries, they were united, enthusiastic, and confident. It had taken time for discipline and organization to become perfectly established throughout their masses, more especially because the labor had fallen almost exclusively upon one man. For Jefferson had been obliged to assume the task with very little assistance. Burr alone, in New York, had proved a really able political lieutenant. At last, however, by tactics and policy intangible and indescribable but wonderfully efficient, the immense multitudes which constituted the Republican raw material had been moulded into an irresistible array, and he who had done this feat still justly enjoys the reputation of being the ablest political leader who has ever lived in this country. The secret of Jefferson's control of the ignorant populace was undoubtedly his honest faith in them; they instinctively felt that his profession of belief in the lower two thirds of the community was genuine; in return they gave gratitude and confidence, and for years patiently submitted to the drill, which he conducted with admirable temper and untiring perseverance. Thus he had now at length made them an invincible body, accomplishing in politics with the voters of the United States very much the same thing that Napoleon was doing in military matters with the untutored militia of France, inspiring them with the irresistible spirit of victory.

This comparative condition of the two parties was so well understood that no intelligent observer was surprised at the result of the elections. There had been some talk of the old manœuvre of withdrawing a few Federalist votes from Adams in order to bring in Charles C. Pinckney ahead of him; but the leaders became aware of the peril of their situation in time to shun this folly. There had also been some danger that a few Republican votes might be thrown away, in order to prevent the occurrence of a tie between the two Republican candidates. On December 15 Jefferson wrote: "Decency required that I should be so entirely passive during the late contest, that I never once asked whether arrangements had been made to prevent so many from dropping votes intentionally as might frustrate half the Republican wish; nor did I doubt, till lately, that such had been made." In spite of this protestation, it is altogether incredible that a party led by Jefferson would ever have been permitted to lapse into so unpardonable a blunder as that which had made him Vice-President, especially after the palpable warning of that occurrence. In fact, when the time came neither party wasted any strength, and the votes of the electoral colleges showed for Jefferson 73 votes, for Burr 73, for Adams 65, for C. C. Pinckney 64, for Jay 1. The equality between Jefferson and Burr of course cast the election into the House of Representatives.

A period of extreme anxiety had now to be endured, scarcely more by Jefferson than by the whole people of the United States. For the political composition of the House was such that the Republicans could not control the choice, and the Federalists, though of course still more unable to do so, yet had the power by holding steadily together to prevent any election whatsoever. Momentous as such a political crime would be, nevertheless many influential Federalists soon showed themselves sufficiently embittered and vindictive to contemplate it. "Several of the high-flying Federalists," wrote Jefferson, December 15, 1800, "have expressed their determination . . . to prevent a choice by the House of Representatives . . . and let the government devolve on a President of the Senate." This threat naturally produced "great dismay and gloom on the Republican gentlemen here, and exultation in the Federalists, who openly declare they . . . will name a President of the Senate *pro tem.* by what they say would only be a *stretch* of the Constitution." Some Federalists asserted that even anarchy was preferable to the success of Jefferson. December 31, Jefferson wrote: "We do not see what is to be the end of the present difficulty. The Federalists . . . propose to prevent an election in Congress, and to transfer the government by an act to the Chief Justice [Jay] or Secretary of State [Marshall], or to let it devolve on the Secretary *pro tem.* of the Senate till next December, which gives them another year's predominance and the chances of future events. The Republicans propose to press forward to an election. If they fail in this, a concert between the two higher candidates may prevent the dissolution of the government and danger of anarchy, by an operation bungling indeed and imperfect, but better than letting the Legislature take the nomination of the Executive entirely from the people." This "operation" was explained, after the crisis had passed, as follows: "I have been above all things solaced by the prospect which opened on us in the event of a non-election of a President, in which case the federal government would have been in the situation of a clock or watch run down. There was no idea of force, nor of any occasion for it. A convention, invited by the Republican members of Congress, with the virtual President and Vice-President, would have been on the ground in eight weeks, would have repaired the Constitution where it was defective, and wound it up again." It was easy for Jefferson to write thus tranquilly and to settle a terrible jeopardy by an obvious simile, after the substantial peril had passed away and he had been occupying the presidential chair for upwards of a fortnight. But it was most fortunate for the country that he and his friends were not driven to this "peaceable and legitimate resource;" they would hardly have succeeded in such an extra-constitutional process of national watch-winding in the teeth of the daring and vindictive men who led the powerful Federal minority. Still worse would it have been for the existence of the infant nation if force had been resorted to, of which there was some threatening talk if the scheme of making Jay or Marshall President should be seriously undertaken. "If they could have been permitted," wrote Jefferson, "to pass a law for putting the government into the hands of an officer, they would certainly have prevented an election. But we thought it best to declare openly and firmly, once for all, that the day such an act passed, the Middle States would arm, and that no such usurpation, even for a single day, should be submitted to. This first shook them; and they were completely alarmed at the resource for which we declared, to wit, a convention to reorganize the government and to amend it. The very word 'convention' gives them the horrors." These letters present an example of the contradictions into which Jefferson was constantly led by his unconquerable passion for construing facts to suit his purpose or feelings of the moment. If it was so seriously threatened that "the Middle States would arm," that the Federalists were overawed by the threat, he was not justified in complacently saying that there was "no idea of force nor of any occasion for it." It was his disingenuous way of making any allegation which would redound to the credit of his party and his political creed.

Perhaps through a fear of some of the consequences above indicated, or perhaps by reason of a revival of good sense and patriotic feeling among the Federalist leaders, the more extravagant plans were gradually superseded by a project marked by nothing worse than petty malice. Before the voting in the House was begun, the Federalists had determined to rest content with the

personal defeat of Jefferson. Though the electors could not designate which of the two persons for whom they voted they intended
for President and which for Vice-President, yet it was perfectly well
known that the whole Republican party had been of one mind in
designing the first place for Jefferson. Indeed, for this position Burr
would have been by no means even their second choice; it was not
without reluctance and hesitation that they had brought themselves to give him the vice-presidency, as the price of his local
influence. But the Federalists, of course, cared not at all for these
facts; they only cherished a hatred and fear of Jefferson propor-
tioned to the love and trust felt towards him by the Republicans.
To throw him out would seem half a victory; and further, many
Federalists would have been so much pleased to see Adams
defeated, that they would have been almost reconciled to the success of a Republican candidate really undesired by his own party. A
revenge, which hurt so many of those whom they disliked, seemed
likely to tempt the anti-Adams Federalists beyond their strength of
resistance. Happily they were stayed from the immediate accomplishment of the plan by the impossibility of so dividing the
Republican members as to effect the necessary combinations; and
during this fortunate delay strong influences were at work to save
the party from the stigma of such disgraceful conduct. Hamilton
strenuously and nobly exerted the great authority which he still
wielded, and though at first few would listen to him, yet in time his
wonderful force triumphed again as it had so often done in years
gone by. It is one of the strangest tales that history has to tell, that
Alexander Hamilton was a chief influence in making Thomas
Jefferson President of the United States. In so doing, the great
Federalist acted from a strict sense of duty, not from any good-will
towards Jefferson personally, and perhaps this fact absolved
Jefferson from any sense of gratitude, which certainly he never
manifested in the faintest degree, even in a negative way. Upon the
seventh day of the balloting, February 17, 1801, the long anxiety

which had weighed terribly not more upon Jefferson individually than upon the people of the whole country, was brought to an end. The Federalist representative from Vermont absented himself; the two Federalists from Maryland put in blank ballots. So ten States, a sufficient number, voted for Jefferson for President. No one, as Jefferson declared with some pleasure, had changed sides; the result had been achieved not by apostate votes but by the more agreeable process of abstention. The Constitution had passed through a strain of such severity as it has never but once since then encountered. The recurrence of the danger was soon averted by an amendment providing that henceforth the electors should designate in their ballots their choice for President and for Vice-President.

Federalist writers have alleged that "terms" were made with Jefferson before his election was permitted to take place. But this assertion, intended to cast a blot upon his behavior, has the most insignificant foundation, if, indeed, it has any at all. He himself said, February 15, 1801, "I have declared to them unequivocally, that I would not receive the government on capitulation, that I would not go into it with my hands tied." He did not do so. He was not a man who could ever have been induced to such a transaction. The most that passed, if anything at all did really pass, was a statement made by one of his friends that, if elected, he did not intend to set himself to overthrow all the important Federalist legislation of the past twelve years, or to make a clean sweep of Federalist incumbents from government offices. That this exposition of his eminently proper intentions could bring any reassurance to the Federalists only shows how absurdly they were frightened. Jefferson had been through a trying ordeal in a very honorable and clean-handed way; and in obtaining the presidency he got no more than he was righteously entitled to.

Burr came out as badly as Jefferson came well. He had been perfectly willing to acquire the presidency by the foul means of a

Federal alliance, in direct contravention of the well-known wishes
of his own party. A more gross betrayal of confidence could hardly
be conceived, even in political life. He had made it clear that his
heart was set upon personal aggrandizement and not upon a
Republican success. His untrustworthiness appeared the more des-
picable by comparison with the strictly honorable conduct of
Jefferson, who might have excused endeavors on his own behalf
upon the plausible ground that he was only forwarding the avowed
will of the party. The antipathy with which many persons had long
since learned to regard Burr now became the sentiment of all honest and intelligent men in the nation. The time was not far distant
when he was sorely to need faithful friends; but his conduct in
these days of temptation had alienated all upright men. His behavior was the more base because Jefferson had behaved handsomely
towards him throughout, and, while the question was still unset-
tled, wrote to him that "it was to be expected that the enemy
would endeavor to sow tares between us, that they might divide us
and our friends. Every consideration satisfies me that you will be
on your guard against this, as I assure you I am strongly." But however Jefferson might deprecate quarrels in the party, both on political and personal considerations, it was not in human nature that his
faith in Burr should not be gravely impaired, and his private
good-will towards such an unscrupulous competitor completely
undermined.

CHAPTER XIII

PRESIDENT: FIRST TERM—
OFFICES—CALLENDER

ON THE EVENING of March 3, 1801, being the last day of Federalist domination in the United States, the functionaries of the moribund party were busy in a not very reputable way. President Adams was making Federalist nominations to official positions, and sending them in to the Senate, which was rapidly confirming them, and John Marshall, Secretary of State, was signing commissions with zealous dispatch. The hour of midnight came upon him while thus employed, and a dramatic tale represents Levi Lincoln, who was to be Attorney-General under Jefferson, walking into Marshall's office, with Mr. Jefferson's watch in his hand, and staying this process of office-filling precisely at twelve o'clock, though many unsigned commissions still lay on the table. This behavior of the Federalists would have been unhandsome enough under any circumstances, but was rendered doubly so by the fact that they professed to regard Jefferson as pledged not to interfere with the persons whom he should find occupying governmental posts at his accession. Adams added his own little personal insult by driving out of Washington during the night, in order to avoid the spectacle of the following day. In one sense of the word that spectacle was sufficiently extraordinary to be worth seeing, for Jefferson had resolved that no pageant should give the lie to his democratic principles, and accordingly he rode on horseback, clad in studiously plain clothes, without attendants, to the capitol, dismounted, tied his horse to the fence, and walked unceremoniously into the senate chamber. There he delivered his inaugural address, an effusion rhetorical to excess and breathing boundless philanthropy. One can read between the lines of his declamatory harangue the conviction of the speaker that his accession to office marked the opening of a glorious epoch in human progress. When he had concluded the delivery he was sworn into office by the Chief Justice of the Supreme Court, and the simple business was over.

This careful abstinence from display marked the new President's whole official career, and at times was carried to an extreme which was, perhaps, even more pretentious and ill-judged than was the contrary fashion which he so pointedly endeavored to condemn. For instance, when Mr. Merry, the British minister; was to be presented, and went "in full official costume" at the appointed day and hour, in company with Mr. Madison, the Secretary of State, to the presidential mansion, he was astonished by a scene which he described as follows : —

> On arriving at the hall of audience we found it empty, at which Mr. Madison seemed surprised, and proceeded to an entry leading to the President's study. I followed him, supposing the introduction was to take place in the adjoining room. At this moment Mr. Jefferson entered the entry at the other end, and all three of us were packed in this narrow space, from which, to make room, I was obliged to back out. In this awkward position my introduction to the President was made by Mr. Madison. Mr. Jefferson's appearance soon explained to me that the general circumstances of my reception had not been accidental, but studied. I, in my official costume, found myself, at the hour of reception he had himself appointed, introduced to a man as the President of the United States, not merely in an undress, but actually standing in slippers

> down at the heels, and both pantaloons, coat, and under-
> clothes indicative of utter slovenliness and indifference to
> appearances, and in a state of negligence actually studied.

This was the ostentation of simplicity; and whether it shall be thought better than the ostentation of ceremonial is a mere question of the form in which personal vanity happens to be developed; though Jefferson preferred to exalt it into matter of principle. But beyond being an affectation, it had, in this instance at least, a serious effect; for it incensed the minister, who "could not doubt that the whole scene was prepared and intended as an insult, not, perhaps, to himself personally, but to the sovereign whom he represented." Jefferson's object, however, was not to please either Mr. Merry or George III; he aimed his dress and deportment at that section of society in which his constituents were chiefly to be found, and with the skill of a good actor he divined accurately the taste of his audience.

When Jefferson was Vice-President he had said: "The second office of the government is honorable and easy, the first is but a splendid misery." From the foregoing anecdotes it may be conceived that he succeeded in escaping the splendor, and upon the misery he certainly entered in a remarkably cheerful frame of mind. He was justified in doing so, since, in respect alike of the foreign and domestic outlook, he had every reason to anticipate a tranquil and prosperous administration. Not only was his party dominant for the time, but he could distinctly foresee that it was likely to retain and increase its power through many years to come. In this ruling party he was supreme; he intended that his sway should be gentle, reasonable, and beneficent, but he knew that it would be none the less absolute because his own moderation might hold it free from the traditional evil characteristics of a despotism. Beneath such genial influences his philanthropic goodwill towards mankind expanded liberally. All his thoughts and words were of

comprehensive love and universal benevolence. He designed to be
master of a political menagerie in which Federalist lions should lie
down peacefully among his flocks of Republican lambs, and only a
very few irredeemable "monarchist" snakes would have to be shut
up in a secure cage by themselves. "My hope," he said, "is that the
distinction will be soon lost, or, at most, that it will be only of
republican and monarchist; that the body of the nation, even that
part which French excesses forced over to the Federal side, will
rejoin the Republicans; leaving only those who were pure monarchists, and who will be too few to form a sect." Amid the exalted
sentiments of his florid inaugural address he declared that "every
difference of opinion is not a difference of principle. We have
called by different names brethren of the same principle. We are all
republicans—we are all federalists. . . . Let us, then, with courage
and confidence, pursue our own federal and republican principles,
our attachment to our Union, and representative government."

In the like spirit he sought in his private utterances to erase all
dividing lines, and to produce an harmonious coalition of both parties. A fortnight before his inauguration, he acknowledged that the
behavior of certain Federalist representatives during the election
must be construed as a "declaration of war." "But," he said, "their
conduct appears to have brought over to us the whole body of
Federalists, who, being alarmed with the danger of a dissolution of
the government, had been made most anxiously to wish the very
administration they had opposed, and to view it, when obtained, as
a child of their own." A few days later he said again of the
Federalists: "These people (I always exclude their leaders) are now
aggregated with us; they look with a certain degree of affection and
confidence to the administration, ready to become attached to it, if
it avoids in the outset acts which might revolt and throw them off.
To give time for a perfect consolidation seems prudent." March 14
he says that the many citizens who had been thrown into a panic by
the revolutionary movements in Europe had "pretty thoroughly

recovered," and "the recovery bids fair to be complete, and to obliterate entirely the line of party division which had been so strongly drawn. Not that their leaders have come over, or ever can come over. But they stand at present almost without followers."

Jefferson was notoriously a political visionary, and this Utopia of harmony was only one among many day-dreams. Yet it was rather an exaggeration of the facts than an invention. For he was really a shrewd observer, though with a sanguine temperament; and in the structures which his imagination reared the blocks were all actualities. Thus, now, he was perfectly right in his prediction that his party was destined to absorb the great bulk of the nation, and to enjoy an ascendency so complete and so long as to produce nearly all the practical effects of a universal fusion of opinions. If it was to the credit of his ability as a statesman that he so surely foresaw this future, it was no less to the credit of his heart that he anticipated it in no spirit of ungenerous triumph. His gratification was honorable and patriotic, with little tinge of selfishness and none of malignity. His joy was for the people rather than for himself, and was really based on the establishment of sound principles more than on his own elevation. On August 26, 1801, he wrote, "the moment which should convince me that a healing of the nation into one is impracticable would be the last moment of my wishing to remain where I am." To this noble end he bent all his thoughts and efforts. The mass of the Federalists, he said, "now find themselves separated from their quondam leaders. If we can but avoid shocking their feelings by unnecessary acts of severity against their late friends, they will in a little time cement and form one mass with us, and by these means harmony and union be restored to our country, which would be the greatest good we could effect."

The indications of success in this grand endeavor were from time to time hailed by Jefferson in a gladsome spirit. New England had always been the stronghold of ultra Federalism, an Egyptian realm of political darkness, according to his notions. In his letter of

June 1, 1798, already quoted, concerning the folly of secession,* he had written: "Seeing that we must have somebody to quarrel with, I had rather keep our New England associates for that purpose than to see our bickerings transferred to others. They are circumscribed within such narrow limits, and their population so full that their numbers will ever be the minority, and they are marked with such a perversity of character as to constitute, from that circumstance, the natural division of our parties." But by May 3, 1801, he was noting with delight symptoms of improving intelligence even in this obnoxious region. "A new subject of congratulation has arisen," he said, "I mean the regeneration of Rhode Island. I hope it is the beginning of that resurrection of the genuine spirit of New England which rises for life eternal. According to natural order, Vermont will emerge next, because least, after Rhode Island, under the yoke of hierocracy." It was the preachers of New England, much accustomed to meddle in matters political, whom Jefferson regarded as the most dangerous enemies of sound doctrines. "From the clergy," he declared, "I expect no mercy. They crucified their Saviour, who preached that their kingdom was not of this world; and all who practice on that precept must expect the extreme of their wrath. The laws of the present day withhold their hands from blood; but lies and slander still remain to them." Yet, in spite of these misguiding obstructionists, the time was not far distant when Massachusetts herself was to become for a time a Republican State. After he had been President a single year Jefferson was able to say: "Our majority in the House of Representatives has been almost two to one; in the Senate, eighteen to fifteen. After another election it will be of two to one in the Senate, and it would not be for the public good to have it greater. . . . The candid Federalists acknowledge that their party can never more raise its head." But he wisely added: "We shall now be so strong that we shall certainly

---

*Ante, p. 194.

split again; . . . but it must be under another name; that of Federalism is become so odious that no party can rise under it."

This result had been greatly furthered by Jefferson's wise moderation in the matter of removals from office. He has been accused of having planted the villainous seed which has since grown into the huge wickedness of the so-called "spoils system," but the charge is unjustifiable. The conduct of the Federalists in the matter of filling offices prior to his inauguration gave him such provocation and excuse as would have induced many men to set about an extensive proscription. He did nothing of the kind, but on the contrary behaved with a liberality towards his opponents which has never been rivalled by any of his successors, save only John Quincy Adams, and which since the evil days of Andrew Jackson would be regarded as nothing less than quixotic. On February 14, 1801, in reply to a letter concerning this interesting subject, he wrote: "No man who has conducted himself according to his duties would have anything to fear from me, as those who have done ill would have nothing to hope, be their political principles what they might. . . . The Republicans have been excluded from all offices from the first origin of the division into Republican and Federalist. They have a reasonable claim to vacancies till they occupy their due share." The righteousness of this proposition could hardly be controverted, and Jefferson was justified in expecting the "justice and good sense of the Federalists" to induce them to "concur in the fairness of the position, that after they have been in the exclusive possession of all offices from the very first origin of party among us to the 3d of March at nine o'clock in the night, no Republican ever admitted, . . . it is now perfectly just that the Republicans should come in for the vacancies which may fall in, until something like an equilibrium in office be restored."

The serious question, however, was not how vacancies should be filled, but how they should be created; whether the gradual operation of deaths, resignations, and expirations of terms of office should be awaited, or whether numerous removals should be made. Jefferson met this problem at once, boldly and frankly. Removals "must be as few as possible, done gradually, and bottomed on some malversation or inherent disqualification." One class only of Federalist incumbents and appointees were to be cleanly swept away, *en masse*, and with unquestionable propriety. These were "the new appointments which Mr. Adams crowded in with whip and spur from the 12th of December, when the event of the election was known, and consequently that he was making appointments not for himself but for his successor, until nine o'clock of the night at twelve o'clock of which he was to go out of office. This outrage on decency should not have its effect, except in the life appointments; . . . as to the others I consider the nominations as nullities." "Official mal-conduct" was of course added as an undeniably proper cause of removal. Otherwise "good men, to whom there is no objection but a difference of political principle, practised on only as far as the right of a private citizen will justify, are not proper subjects of removal." The only exception which Jefferson was inclined to make to this rule was "in the case of attorneys and marshals." Since the courts were "decidedly federal and irremovable," he believed "that Republican attorneys and marshals, being the doors of entrance into the courts, are indispensably necessary as a shield to the Republican part of our fellow-citizens which, I believe, is the main body of the people." Though it is needless to say that the Judiciary department was both honest and able, yet there was fair ground for a Republican to entertain this jealousy and distrust towards it. The Supreme Court, by virtue of its power to construe the new Constitution, was of scarcely less political importance than the Executive. Yet the judges of all the courts of the United States, the district attorneys and the marshals, almost to a man, were Federalists, and undeniably, also, most of them were partisans in their temper. Even a new and superfluous body of judges had been recently created by the Federal Congress, and all the seats had been filled by Mr. Adams with strong friends of his own, holding of course by a life tenure. Very properly this extra bench was abolished by the Republican Congress shortly after Mr. Jefferson's accession. But the other courts could not be abolished with equal propriety, and the attorneyships and marshalships could only be emptied by removals. There was abundant justification for Jefferson's assertion that the Republican party ought to have some foothold in the great and omnipresent department of justice. The desire to base removals upon official misconduct doubtless induced an extreme readiness to believe vague and doubtful charges, such, for example, as the common one of "packing juries;" but this signified only a wish to throw a cloak of decency about a transaction not substantially blameworthy.

Upon such principles concerning offices did Jefferson start, principles which he not only professed in words but carried out in practice. In time, as he came to feel a little more accustomed to exercise power, and perhaps a trifle weary of resisting importunities, he modified his views a little, but only a little, for the worse. His real kindness of heart made it always disagreeable to him to turn any one out of office; he spoke of it as "a dreadful operation to perform," a "painful operation." He suspected that "the heaping of abuse on me personally has been with the design and the hope of provoking me to make a general sweep of all Federalists out of office," to the end that thus he might be rendered unpopular and the Federalist party regain through persecution the consolidation which it was so rapidly losing. "But," he said, "as I have carried no passion into the execution of this disagreeable duty, I shall suffer none to be excited." After he had been somewhat more than two years in office, he wrote: "Some removals, to wit, sixteen, to the end of our first session of Congress, were made on political principles alone, in very urgent cases; and we determined to make no more but for delinquency or active and bitter opposition to the order of things which the public will had established. On this last ground nine were removed from the end of the first to the end of the second session of Congress; and one since that. So that sixteen [twenty-six?] only have been removed in the whole for political principles, that is to say, to make room for some participation for the Republicans." On May 30, 1804, he was willing to state as a cause for removal, "that the patronage of public offices should no longer be confided to one who uses it for active opposition to the national will," which, of course, was only a clever way of describing hostility to the dominant party. Yet it must be admitted that Jefferson never drifted far from the honorable doctrines which he first proclaimed, and that he showed great courage and honesty in permitting their offices to be retained by the mass of incumbents belonging to a party which had rigidly proscribed Republicans. Had positions been reversed, it is rather to be hoped than asserted that a Federalist President would have emulated this conduct of the Republican leader. Among the removals which Jefferson did make was that of John Quincy Adams from the place of commissioner of bankruptcy at Boston. The Federalists regarded this as a very petty manifestation of personal malice; but Jefferson afterward, in a letter to Mrs. John Adams, apparently in reply to her reproaches, declared that he was ignorant that Mr. Adams held the position when he caused the place to be vacated.

In the important and very difficult matter of selecting appointees President Jefferson acted with painstaking conscientiousness. "There is nothing," he said, "that I am so anxious about as good nominations." "No duty . . . is more difficult to fulfil. The knowledge of characters possessed by a single individual is, of necessity, limited." Accordingly he begs friends in whom he can trust to aid him with information. Sometimes, though apparently very seldom, he made mistakes. He was severely attacked for giving the collectorship of New Haven to one Samuel Bishop, who was said to be grossly incapacitated by old ago; but he defended the appointment with very plausible justifications. We never find him treating past political services as a recommendation to office, and he rigorously condemned any active interference in politics by the incumbents of federal offices. February 2, 1801, he wrote: "One thing I will say, that as to the future, interferences with elections, whether of the state or general government, by officers of the latter, should be deemed cause for removal; because the constitutional remedy by the elective principle becomes nothing, if it may be smothered by the enormous patronage of the federal government." He afterward treated "electioneering activity, and open and industrious opposition to the principles of the present government," as among the proper causes for removing Federalists from office. But the rules which he enforced against Federalist placemen he laid down equally against Republican incumbents, and carried into effect as far probably as could be fairly expected. In September, 1804, he notified the Secretary of the Treasury that "the officers of the federal government are meddling too much with the public elections. Will it be best to admonish them privately or by proclamation? This for consideration till we meet."

The Federalist newspapers were far from reciprocating the generosity displayed by Jefferson towards the office-holders of their party. It is to this period that the pitiful story of Callender's malicious defamation belongs. This miserable fellow was a Scotchman by birth, but had been compelled to seek refuge in this country in order to escape prosecution for the contents of a pamphlet which he had written concerning "The Political Progress of Great Britain." In the United States he brought his pen to the service of the Republican party. At first Jefferson esteemed him an able and useful writer; for his assaults, though coarse, were forcible; and he was willing to say vigorously things which persons of higher position were not unwilling to have said by others on their behalf. Morally he was a thoroughly low and contemptible creature, utterly devoid of any restraints of honor or decency. It was he who first got upon the scent of Hamilton's amour with Mrs. Reynolds, and at once published the evidence which he had dishonorably secured; and it was he who wrote the most infamous of those attacks upon Washington which were, in the opinion not only of contemporaries, but of posterity, the preëminently unjustifiable and unpardonable offence of the new party. As his scurrility increased, his ability diminished; while of discretion he was utterly void. Soon his diatribes degenerated to the low level to be expected from a political hack-writer who was also an habitual drunkard. Jefferson, according to his own account, became heartily disgusted with a protégé who had become mischievous as well as repulsive, and would have given more to stop so impious a pen than to keep it moving. Yet, whether from softness of heart, as he protested, or from a secret gratification at the work Callender was doing, as the Federalists charged, Jefferson continued from time to time to assist the wretch with small sums of money.

Under Adams' administration Callender had the good fortune to become a martyr, being one of half a dozen defendants who were found guilty, imprisoned, and fined under the Sedition law. Jefferson, as soon as he came into office, remitted the short remainder of the term of imprisonment, and caused the fine to be repaid, "by a somewhat doubtful exercise of power," as the Federalists very properly said. But Jefferson considered the Sedition law "to be a nullity, as absolute and as palpable as if Congress had ordered us to fall down and worship a golden image; and that it was as much [his] duty to arrest its execution in every stage as it would have been to have rescued from the fiery furnace those who should have been cast into it for refusing to worship the image." Despite his dread of embroilments, Jefferson never shirked the responsibilities imposed upon him by such strong convictions; and Callender now had the advantage of the President's courage, as before of his liberality. But a nature more greedy than grateful only hungered for additional favors. The liberated man hastened to urge the President to remove the postmaster at Richmond and give him the office. The postmaster was a Federalist editor, but Jefferson very honorably refused to displace him. For this behavior he speedily suffered in a fashion which certainly hardly encourages men in public life to be scrupulously upright. Callender immediately allied himself with the editorial staff of the Richmond "Recorder," and filled that paper, day after day, with countless stories—partly his own, partly contributed by others—derogatory to Jefferson. The sheet, hitherto a petty local publication, quickly found its way to the remotest corners of the country; for Callender's characteristic onslaught was of the most ignoble, but certainly of the most effective kind. He charged Jefferson with having been his friend and financial assistant, and his confederate in the libels upon Washington; but his chief topic was Jefferson's private life, and his many tales were scandalous and revolting to the last degree. Naturally these slanders will not bear repetition here; for they were worse than mere charges of simple amours. Apart from the fact that no decent man would have wished to dip his hands in such filth, one would think that the transaction which had instigated Callender to this conduct would have induced any Federalist editor of moderately good feeling to discountenance so base a revenge. At least these gentlemen might have remembered that they had lately stigmatized Callender as a low and untrustworthy liar, when Hamilton and Washington had been his victims. But, to the discredit of the journalists of that period, it must be confessed that their conduct was contrary both to gratitude and to decency. Every Federalist writer hastened to draw for his own use bucketful after bucketful from Callender's foul reservoir, and the gossip about Jefferson's graceless debaucheries was sent into every household in the United States. Jefferson never undertook to deny any of these narratives; and Federalist historians, from whom a fairer judgment might have been expected, have seen fit to treat this silence as evidence of guilt. Obviously it was not so. The President of the United States could hardly stoop to give the lie to a fellow like Callender, especially in such a department of calumny. It would be pleasanter for us also to have ignored the matter; but this was scarcely possible, since the charges gravely affected Jefferson's happiness and reputation at the time, and have ever since been repeated to his discredit by writers upon that period. He will probably always be thought of as a man who carried licentiousness far beyond the limit which a grateful nation has tried hard to condone in the cases of Franklin, Hamilton, and many another among the sages and patriots even of those virtuous and simple days. Nevertheless there is no sufficient and unquestionable proof that Jefferson was one whit worse than the majority of his compeers. Nor is it probable that any one would ever have thought him so if he could have brought himself to make a political removal and appointment such as in these days would be regarded as matter of course.

CHAPTER XIV

PRESIDENT: FIRST TERM—LOUISIANA

JEFFERSON HAD A fair measure of respect for the Constitution,— perhaps a little more than is ordinarily felt towards a common statute. He was far from regarding it with a blind homage, as if it were the sacred principle of the national life. This was not alone attributable to the facts that tradition had not yet lent to it a sort of consecration, and that prosperity beneath it had not endured long enough to give it a reputation; the feeling was more largely due to Jefferson's abstract views concerning government. A constitution might too often have the effect of fetters upon the nation. The will of the people, which had made the Constitution, might at any time modify or abrogate it. That will ought to be the ultimate rule of decision in any matter sufficiently momentous to justify an appeal to it. Therefore, if the will of the people was with him in an unconstitutional policy which he believed to be sound, Jefferson did not hesitate to speak respectfully of the Constitution, and to disregard it. Perhaps he is the only President of the United States who has ever avowedly and with premeditation carried through an important extra-constitutional measure, relying for justification simply upon the wisdom of the act and the wish of the nation. Such was the real character of his purchase of Louisiana.

From the first moment, many years before the time with which we are now dealing, when his attention had been called to the rights of the United States concerning the Mississippi River,

Jefferson had been fully alive to their vast importance. Indeed his estimate of the probable traffic upon that stream, and the consequent growth of New Orleans as a commercial metropolis, has since appeared exaggerated, at least in comparison with the proportionate growth of the rest of the country. In the summer of 1790 a rupture between England and Spain seemed imminent, and Jefferson promptly made ready to seize the opportune moment for compelling a settlement of the open question of navigation. Spain owned both sides of the mouth of the river; but the United States had always asserted that this ownership gave the Spaniards no right to close the stream to the free passage of American vessels. In August, 1790, Jefferson, being then Secretary of State, wrote a vigorous letter to Carmichael, the representative of the United States at the Court of Madrid. He directed that gentleman to impress the Spanish minister "thoroughly with the necessity of an early and even an immediate settlement of this matter;" though "a resumption of the negotiation is not desired on our part, unless he can determine, in the opening of it, to yield the immediate and full enjoyment of that navigation." But if this point was to be yielded in the outset, what further subject for negotiation remained? Jefferson boldly said that it was "a port, where the sea and river vessels may meet and exchange loads, and where those employed about them may be safe and unmolested." There must be no dallying about this business, he added, since "it is impossible to answer for the forbearance of our Western citizens. We endeavor to quiet them with an expectation of an attainment of their ends by peaceable means. But should they, in a moment of impatience, hazard others, there is no saying how far we may be led; for neither themselves nor their rights will ever be abandoned by us."

With an admirable zeal and persistence Jefferson pushed this demand for many months. He rapidly developed his notion concerning the port; he declared the obvious necessity that it should "be so well separated from the territories of Spain and her jurisdiction as not to engender daily disputes and broils between us," such as must inevitably "end in war." "Nature," he then cleverly added, "has decided what shall be the geography of that in the end, whatever it might be in the beginning, by cutting off from the adjacent countries of Florida and Louisiana, and inclosing between two of its channels, a long and narrow slip of land, called the Island of New Orleans." He admitted that this audacious proposition "could not be hazarded to Spain in the first step; it would be too disagreeable at first view; because this island, with its town, constitutes at present their principal settlement in that part of their dominions." But he cheerfully reflected that "reason and events may by little and little familiarize them to it." He was right; in due time "reason and events," having had the way opened for them by the diplomatic skill and pertinacity of the Secretary of State, did familiarize the Spanish Court with this "idea." The right of navigation was conceded by the treaty of 1795, and with it a right to the free use of the port of New Orleans upon reasonably satisfactory terms for a period of three years, and thereafterward until some other equally convenient harbor should be allotted. The credit of this ultimate achievement was Mr. Jefferson's, none the less because the treaty was not signed until he had retired from office. It was really his statesmanship which had secured it, not only in spite of the natural repugnance of Spain, but also in spite of the obstacles indirectly thrown in his way in the earlier stages by many persons in the United States, who privately gave the Spanish minister to understand that the country cared little about the Mississippi, and would not support the Secretary in his demands.

It is curious to note that in the course of this business there was already a faint foreshadowing of that principle, which many years afterwards was christened with the name of Monroe. For a brief time it was thought, not without reason, that so soon as hostilities should break out between England and Spain, the former power would seize upon the North American possessions of the latter.

Jefferson wrote to Gouverneur Morris: "We wish you, therefore, to intimate to them (the British ministry) that we cannot be indifferent to enterprises of this kind. That we should contemplate a change of neighbors with extreme uneasiness. That a due balance on our borders is not less desirable to us than a balance of power in Europe has always appeared to them."

The arrangements at last consummated in 1795 remained in force, working fairly well, for many years. But the wiser men in the United States were not so much satisfied as they were biding their time to get a more permanent foothold. In 1802–3 the opportunity came, certainly by a very peculiar introduction. So early as 1790 there had been suspicions that France would like to regain her possessions on the Gulf of Mexico. Thus at that time Jefferson, though seeking French aid to assist him in enforcing the demands of the United States against Spain, had been afraid to expose the full extent of his designs; for, he said, "it is believed here that the Count de Moustier, during his residence with us, conceived the project of again engaging France in a colony upon our continent, and that he directed his views to some of the country on the Mississippi, and obtained and communicated a good deal of matter on the subject to his court." For some years afterward the project slept, but rumors of like purport started into fresh life early in 1800. Apparently these gave at first little serious uneasiness, though later in the year instructions were sent to the American ministers at London, Paris, and Madrid to do all in their power to prevent any cession of territory by Spain to France. Interference, however, came too late. Before the instructions reached our ministers the deed had been done. On October 1, 1800, Spain ceded all Louisiana to France. The treaty, however, was kept secret for a while, so that not until the spring of 1802 did it become really known in the United States as an assured fact. Jefferson then was profoundly chagrined. He appreciated more fully than any other public man of the day the immeasurable value of that region to the

States; and he was proportionately disturbed to see it pass from weak into strong hands.

The vexation felt by Jefferson, in his public capacity, might have been partially allayed by a consolation afforded to him as an individual. For the situation at least gave him an opportunity to clear his character from the aspersions of those Federalists who had so bitterly accused him of loving France better than his native land. No sooner did he conceive that the interests of the two peoples menaced even a future clashing, than he showed himself thoroughly and zealously American. Instantly his French sympathy dwindled into a feeble expression of regret that France should be transformed from a "natural friend" into a "natural enemy;" for this, he said, was the inevitable consequence of what had occurred. April 18, 1802, he wrote to Robert R. Livingston, minister at Paris:—

> The cession of Louisiana and the Floridas by Spain to France works most sorely on the United States. On this subject the Secretary of State has written to you fully, yet I cannot forbear recurring to it personally, so deep is the impression it makes on my mind. It completely reverses all the political relations of the United States. . . . There is on the globe one single spot, the possessor of which is our natural and habitual enemy. It is New Orleans. . . . It is impossible that France and the United States can continue long friends, when they meet in so irritable a position. . . . We must be very improvident if we do not begin to make arrangements on that hypothesis. The day that France takes possession of New Orleans fixes the sentence which is to restrain her forever within her low water mark. It seals the Union of two nations, who, in conjunction, can maintain exclusive possession of the ocean. From that moment we must marry ourselves to the British fleet and nation.

One almost discredits his own senses as he beholds Jefferson voluntarily proclaiming the banns for these nuptials, which during so many years past would have seemed to him worse than illicit. Yet he was never more in earnest, and betrays a striking solemnity and depth of feeling throughout his letter, while obviously writing under the influence of an unusual excitement. Yet even beneath disappointment he was sanguine, and amid indignation he was diplomatic. "I should suppose," he says, "that all these considerations might, in some proper form, be brought into view of the government of France. Though stated by us it ought not to give offence, because we do not bring them forward as a menace, but as consequences not controllable by us, but inevitable from the course of things." As usual he turns to time as his most efficient ally. The French troops, he says, are to subdue St. Domingo before they cross to receive delivery of Louisiana; and he complacently adds, "the conquest of St. Domingo will not be a short work. It will take considerable time and wear down a great number of soldiers." This interval he hopes to employ well in working upon the French government.

But an untoward event, occurring a few months after the receipt of news of the cession, was near robbing Mr. Jefferson even of such slight possibilities as might be contained in this interval. At this most inopportune moment, in October, 1802, the Spanish Intendant at New Orleans issued an edict, in direct contravention of treaty stipulations, cutting short the American privilege of deposit at that port. At once the hot spirit of the Western country was in a wild blaze. Those pioneers who kept their rifles over their fire-places or behind their front doors, ready to shoot a catamount, an Indian, or each other, at a moment's notice, now talked fiercely of marching straight into New Orleans, and making a prompt settlement with powder and lead. Jefferson was much disturbed by demonstrations which threatened serious interference with a plan which he had conceived. War he rightly deemed the last resource.

A display of warlike spirit might be useful to emphasize his diplomacy; but he was alarmed at the prospect of this temper really bursting into action. Yet he sympathized with the Western men in their wrath, and bore them no grudge, though they seemed so likely to derange his schemes by their uncontrollable zeal.

The persons with whom the President was really vexed, and fairly enough too, it must be confessed, were the Federalists. The remnant of this party now for an instant imagined that they saw a chance of being borne again into power by hostilities with France. Careless of the interests of the country as against the interests of party, they became clamorous for immediate war. Jefferson well described the situation, January 13, 1803:—

> The agitation of the public mind . . . is extreme. In the Western country it is natural, and grounded on honest motives. In the seaports it proceeds from a desire for war, which increases the mercantile lottery; in the Federalists generally, and especially those of Congress, the object is to force us into war if possible, in order to derange our finances; or, if this cannot be done, to attach the Western country to them, as their best friends, and thus get again into power. Remonstrances, memorials, etc., are now circulating through the whole of the Western country, and signed by the body of the people.

But the small and embittered faction into which the Federalist party had rapidly degenerated could not beat Jefferson, intrenched in the confidence of the nation, and backed by a handsome majority in Congress.

In the House of Representatives this majority was imperiously led by John Randolph, whose faith in Jefferson was still blindly implicit. In the latter part of 1802 he carried the House into secret session, against vehement opposition from the Federalists, in order to give the President an opportunity for making certain private communications, and obtaining legislation thereon. Precisely what took place behind the closed doors was never fully divulged; but the substance of the whole work done publicly and privately during a few weeks of that winter was thoroughly satisfactory to the Executive. Many resolutions offered by the Federalists, designed at once to obstruct a peaceable settlement and to win the allegiance of the West by a show of angry zeal, were voted down by loyal majorities. Finally, the management of the whole business was left to the President, who was further provided with the sum of two million dollars, to be used as he should see fit.

Jefferson's plans were by this time well understood to be the purchase of New Orleans, and probably also something more on the east side of the river. He had early adopted this scheme, justly thinking that it would be cheaper, wiser, more humane, in every way more becoming a civilized and mercantile people, to buy the fee of such territory as they needed, rather than to engage in a war simply for the purpose of establishing an easement in an island. The two million dollars were required to pave the way; in other words, to bribe some of the more influential among those virtuous legislators who had succeeded the wicked monarchs of France. Jefferson had already taken initial steps towards this bargain through Livingston at Paris. But that minister, before he had learned the executive purpose, had unfortunately expressed very different views of his own. He had told the French government that the United States cared not at all whether their neighbor at the mouth of the Mississippi was to be France or Spain, provided the right of navigation and privileges of deposit should not be interfered with. After correction, indeed, he began to discuss a purchase, and in time would probably have concluded it; but Jefferson, for many reasons, chose to send a special emissary. Apart from the point of sympathetic conviction, it was desirable to make a show of energy before the West and the Federalists, who had little confidence in Livingston. Further, it was an uncomfortable task to put into the dangerous black and white of diplomatic instructions all which the President wished to say. He accordingly bethought him of Monroe, whose term as Governor of Virginia had just expired, and on February 11, 1803, nominated that gentleman envoy-extraordinary to France. The nomination was promptly confirmed, in spite of the malicious suggestion of the Federalists, who averred that it was made only to provide a place for a personal and political friend, who was in financial difficulties. In sundry interviews with Jefferson, Monroe became fully informed as to the President's projects, and departed on his delicate errand apparently without a word in writing upon which he could rely, should his principal choose later to disavow his doings. But Jefferson's friends always trusted him.

At this same point in the business Jefferson manifested a mercantile cleverness of which any tradesman might have been proud. He wrote to Dupont de Nemours, urging him to smooth the way towards settlement, and throwing out divers shrewd suggestions:— "Our circumstances are so imperious as to admit of no delay as to our course; and the use of the Mississippi is so indispensable that we cannot hesitate one moment to hazard our existence for its maintenance." This for a timely hint of the "dernier ressort." Then he adds:

> It may be said, if this object be so all-important to us, why do we not offer such a sum as to insure its purchase? The answer is simple. We are an agricultural people, poor in money and owing great debts. These will be falling due by instalments for fifteen years to come, and require from us the practice of a rigorous economy to accomplish their payment; and it is our principle to pay to a moment whatever we have engaged, and never to engage what we cannot and mean not faithfully to pay. We have calculated our resources, and find the sum to be

> moderate which they would enable us to pay, and we
> know from late trials that little can be added to it by bor-
> rowing. The country, too, which we wish to purchase, . . .
> is a barren sand. . . . We cannot, then, make anything by
> a sale of the land to individuals. So that it is peace alone
> which makes it an object with us, and which ought to
> make the cession of it desirable to France.

Could an attorney drive a bargain more skilfully? A willing but very poor purchaser, absolutely sure to pay his notes at maturity, shunning discord rather than seeking profit; indirect but valuable advantages to accrue to the seller from the sale, in addition to the price; an unmarketable piece of property; a misty vision of war in the background! Yet, in spite of such plausible persuasions, it is not probable that Monroe would have had much success in his negotiations, had not European politics come opportunely to his aid. Napoleon, who already exercised the powers of an emperor under the title of First Consul, had set his heart upon establishing a great French colony on the North American continent. Under this impulse he had laughed to scorn the first proposals for a purchase of his territory. It would have been easier for Monroe to buy up his advisers than for those advisers to induce him to abandon a favorite whim. Neither was there much use in threatening the conqueror of Europe with the wrath of our trans-Alleghanian population. But as Jefferson's usual good fortune arranged it, by the time Monroe arrived the short-lived peace of Amiens was obviously about to be broken. On the verge of extensive military operations Napoleon forgot his colonial schemes. In the contemplation of a hungry treasury he became as eager to sell as the envoys were to buy. Monroe's instructions had contemplated only a moderate purchase, of the island and some land upon the easterly side of the river, nothing more being thought possible. But Napoleon's notion now was to turn his most available assets into money with all speed. He intimated that he would sell all Louisiana. He asked, indeed, a great price; but where both parties are eager, trading is usually rapid. Monroe had gauged Jefferson's views with perfect accuracy, and felt no fear. In a few days he and Livingston closed the bargain, buying Louisiana outright for sixty million livres, with the stipulation that the United States should pay sundry claims of its merchants against France to the amount of twenty million livres more, and that certain privileges should be allowed to French and Spanish vessels in the port of New Orleans for twelve years to come.

In their dispatches, communicating this treaty, the envoys acknowledged that they had exceeded their instructions, and humbly hoped that they had not erred. This was literally true, but it was only the letter not the spirit of their instructions which had been overstepped. Monroe well knew that he had only fulfilled Jefferson's real wishes. But since this was not apparent on the surface, the Federalists afterward pretended to regard these professions of the negotiators as indicating that any credit there might be in the purchase was due to them rather than to the President. This, however, was an unfair artifice, which at best could amount to nothing more than saying that the presidential policy had succeeded even beyond the hopes of its projector. The entire credit—or discredit, if such there were—of the achievement belonged exclusively to Jefferson.

Of course fault-finding began at once. No great ingenuity was needed on the part of the opposition to devise the gravest objections to the transaction both as a whole and in detail. The government was without constitutional authority to make the purchase upon terms which substantially involved the speedy admission of the purchased territory, in the shape of new States, to the Union. It was directly contrary to the Constitution to grant peculiar privileges in the port of New Orleans to Spanish and French commerce. The boundaries of Louisiana, both upon the east and upon the west, were in dispute, and in time would probably have to be settled by a war. Spain had insisted as a condition of her own transfer that France should not sell; Spain was still in possession and might now well be expected to decline to part with the property. These criticisms each and all were perfectly true; yet they were certainly each and all of very little consequence, when set against an acquisition so enormously valuable in so many different ways to the United States. The practical objections Jefferson met by practical suggestions. The boundaries were doubtful, but boundaries in wild lands constantly remain doubtful for many years without engendering serious hostilities. In this interval, the natural growth of the United States and the inevitable decadence of Spain upon this continent would ultimately insure a peaceful yielding to American demands. A little later he proposed, in pursuance of this view, that the government should offer bounties to attract a large body of vigorous and intelligent American colonists into Louisiana, to the end that a population of such numbers, character, and national sympathies should be established in that quarter as would discourage contumacious neighbors. It would have been better, some said, to have bought the Floridas rather than Louisiana. But could not another purchase be made? The American claims of boundary

> will be a subject of negotiation with Spain, and if, as soon as she is at war, we push them strongly with one hand, holding out a price in the other, we shall certainly obtain the Floridas, and all in good time. . . . Propositions are made to exchange Louisiana, or a part of it, for the Floridas. But, as I have said, we shall get the Floridas without; and I would not give one inch of the waters of the Mississippi to any nation, because I see in a light very important to our peace the exclusive right to its navigation, and the admission of no nation into it but as into the Potomac or Delaware, with our consent and under our police.

Time proved the perfect truth of all this.

As for the chance of Spain refusing to deliver possession to the United States, Jefferson intended to have no trifling in that matter. So soon as the treaty was ratified he

> sent off orders to the Governor of the Mississippi terri-
> tory and General Wilkinson to move down with the
> troops at hand to New Orleans, and receive possession
> from M. Laussat. If he is heartily disposed to carry the
> order of the Consul into execution, he can probably com-
> mand a volunteer force at New Orleans, and will have
> the aid of ours also, if he desires it, to take the possession
> and deliver it to us. If he is not so disposed, we shall take
> the possession, and it will rest with the government of
> France by adopting the act as their own and obtaining
> the confirmation of Spain, to supply the non-execution
> of their agreement to deliver and to entitle themselves to
> the complete execution of our part of the agreements.

For the other objections of law and theory, Jefferson was inclined to override them very cavalierly. In truth it was the only way. It was not worth while to enter into a debate, predestined to obvious defeat, nor to engage in argument when the whole weight of logic rested with the other side. The prompt vote of a silent majority was the best policy. "The less that is said about any con-stitutional difficulty, the better; . . . it will be desirable for Congress to do what is necessary in silence." "Whatever Congress shall think it necessary to do, should be done with as little debate as possible, and particularly so far as respects the constitutional difficulty." Thus Jefferson wrote. The opposition, on the other hand, tried hard to force a prolonged discussion, but with slender effect. The outnumbering administrationists cared not to hear long lectures, designed to show only that a wise act, which they had already determined to do, was against the law. So the Federalist speeches, though calling forth only a few replies and certainly no answers, went for nothing. In the Senate a powerful and delighted Republican majority hastened to ratify the treaty by a vote of twenty-four to seven,—ten votes more than were necessary, as Jefferson triumphantly noted. In the House of Representatives the overwhelming ranks of the same party, under the spirited leadership of Randolph, first made the necessary appropriations, and then provided temporarily for the government of the territory by the President, even giving him for the time all the powers of the late Spanish monarchs, an odd position for Jefferson truly, but which he did not reject.

Thus did Jefferson accomplish a most momentous transaction in direct contravention of all those grand principles which for many years he had been eloquently preaching as the political faith of the great party which he had formed and led. What henceforth could he and his followers say about Washington's aristocratic ceremonial at his levees; what about Hamilton's establishment of a United States Bank; what about all the alleged twistings and wrenchings of the Constitution by the free-constructionists and the "monarchists"? Here was an act, done by the great Republican doctrinaire-president, utterly beyond the Constitution in substance and contrary to it in detail; monarchical, beyond what any "monocrat" had ever dared to dream of. There was no denying these facts, at least without self-stultification. John Randolph, dictating to his great majority in the House, became ridiculous when he endeavored to reconcile the treaty with the organic charter of the United States. The plain truth was that Jefferson had simply shattered into fragments his previous theories, and every one in the United States saw and knew it. In August, 1800, he had declared that "the true theory of our Constitution is surely the wisest and best: that the States are independent as to everything within themselves, and united as to everything respecting foreign nations." By this theory "our general government may be reduced to a very simple organization and a very inexpensive one; a few plain duties to be performed by a few servants." The doctrine of a simple league of independent powers, devised only for the specific purpose of foreign intercourse, could not have been better set forth. Yet it was hardly possible to imagine a transaction more at variance with the principle of such a league than was this purchase of an enormous property for the common tenancy and at the common charge of the political partnership. It produced a welding and unifying of domestic interests to as great an extent as an isolated act could do.

Still more surprising is it to remember that Jefferson was the chief expositor of states' rights. He declares them in the foregoing sentences; he had declared them again and again, in public and private, directly and indirectly. He was the author of the Kentucky resolutions. But the justification upon which he had relied to sustain nullification and secession by Kentucky was as nothing compared to the justification which he himself, by this purchase, now created for nullification and secession on the part of the dissatisfied Eastern States. The Constitution, he had always insisted, was a contract between independent parties, not binding upon any one of them beyond its distinct stipulations. It was not among those stipulations that a majority might purchase new territory, and out of it create and admit new parties to the contract. It was the inevitable outcome of his own logic that any State might now lawfully withdraw from the league upon this opportunity which he himself had furnished.

Yet by a singular inconsistency, which, perhaps, he did not appreciate, he managed to reiterate his old principles, even while he stood among the very ruins into which he had prostrated them. He actually seized this extraordinary moment for an extreme assertion of the doctrine of states' rights, accompanied by some of that mawkish sentimentality and political rubbish which so constantly excite a revulsion of feeling when one most wishes to admire him.

The Federalists, he says, "see in this acquisition the formation of a new Confederacy, embracing all the waters of the Mississippi,

on both sides of it, and a separation of its eastern waters from us."
This result he thinks improbable. But the possibility of its hap-
pening does not appear to him an argument against that purchase
which may promote it. For "the future inhabitants of the Atlantic
and Mississippi States will be our sons. We leave them in distinct
but bordering establishments; we think we see their happiness in
their union, and we wish it. Events may prove it otherwise; and if
they see their interest in separation, why should we take sides
with our Atlantic rather than our Mississippi descendants? It is the
elder and the younger son differing. God bless them both, and
keep them in union, if it be for their good, but separate them if it
be better." This is the piety of states' rights and the statesmanship
of secession, very plausibly put under the peculiar circumstances.
He reiterated it again with something less of holiness in his language about six months later. "Whether we remain one confederacy, or form into Atlantic and Mississippi confederacies, I believe
not very important to the happiness of either part. Those of the
western confederacy will be as much our children and descendants
as those of the eastern," etc. It is inevitable that one pauses a
moment to speculate upon the problem, what gospel Jefferson
would have had to preach to the people in 1861. Would he have
been among those whose text was "Let them go in peace"?
Probably not, for he would have preferred inconsistency to
unpopularity.

Yet these matters of argument and logic, theory and consistency,
may easily be dwelt upon unfairly. For every one must admit that the
government ought to have bought Louisiana, and must equally
admit that the propriety of the purchase did not alone suffice to annihilate all those broad political theories of the Republican party which
would have forbidden it. It was simply a proper case for breaking,
without discrediting, a rule, a case which will occur under any and all
rules. So far as Jefferson personally was concerned, Destiny, that god-

dess who loves nothing so much as irony, had led him to the point to which she so often leads the profoundest statesmen and the wisest philosophers, the point where the choice must be made betwixt a sound abstract doctrine and a sensible act inconsistent therewith. In the dilemma Jefferson did what all really great statesmen and philosophers always have done, and always will do in such an emergency; he turned his back upon the doctrine and did the act. He preferred sound sense to sound logic, and set intelligent statesmanship above political consistency. Of course he laid himself open to reproach and ridicule. Throughout the country every Federalist throat sent forth a howl of abuse against the democrat who had turned autocrat; every Federalist finger was pointed in scorn at the strict constructionist who, in an instant, had thrown overboard the whole Constitution. But Jefferson bore these taunts with much tranquillity. He could afford to do so. If his political philosophy had become somewhat emaciated beneath the severe treatment to which he had subjected it, his popularity as a statesman had waged hugely fat upon the same food. "The treaty," he said, "has obtained nearly general approbation. The Federalists spoke and voted against it; but they are now so reduced in their numbers as to be nothing." Yet he behaved really very well. He did not try to carry off his lawlessness with a high hand, as the applause of the people might have tempted and enabled him to do. He did not endeavor to put upon the transaction any sophistical gloss, which his dialectic cleverness would have made easy for him, especially in the presence of a well-disposed audience. But he frankly acknowledged that the necessities of the case had compelled him to do what was unlawful. Abjuring such sophistries as the administrationists in Congress had put forth, he honestly said, even while the matter was still pending:—

> The Constitution has made no provision for our holding foreign territory, still less for incorporating foreign nations into our Union. The Executive, in seizing the

fugitive occurrence which so much advances the good of
their country, have done an act beyond the Constitution.
The Legislature, in casting behind them metaphysical
subtleties, and risking themselves, like faithful servants,
must ratify and pay for it, and throw themselves on their
country for doing for them unauthorized, what we know
they would have done for themselves had they been in a
situation to do it.

Loath to leave his justification solely to the wisdom of his act,
he desired to be put, technically, in as sound a position as possible.
To this end he was very anxious that there should be a formal rati-
fication by the people in the shape of a constitutional amendment.
He even drew up one, and intimated to his friends in the cabinet
and in Congress that he hoped to see it put upon its passage. They
were less scrupulous than he, and would not concern themselves
much about it, so that it was allowed to drop. Perhaps he was not
so urgent in pushing the scheme as he might have been; but at least
he did not disguise his opinions and his wishes, which were undeniably correct and becoming.

Yet it may be said that in a certain way Jefferson had been true
to his fundamental and grandest principles, even in breaking those
which were in a sense secondary. He believed primarily in the will
of the people, and sought primarily the good of the people. The
Constitution commanded his respect, because it formally
expressed that will and substantially advanced that good. In a
peculiar crisis, where this written law seemed to lose these distinc-
tive characteristics, it seemed also for the time to lose much of its
title to obedience. It was true he had no technical or definite
expression of the people's will, but it would have been absurd to
pretend to doubt that he executed that will in acquiring Louisiana
upon favorable terms, by, against, or outside of the Constitution. If
the necessary constitutional amendment could have been made by

an immediate popular vote, it would have been accomplished in a week. This is a hazardous doctrine, and so was Jefferson's action, though right, a dangerous precedent. But certainly the history of the transaction puts it beyond a question that the statesman predominated over the doctrinaire in his composition, though his enemies to this day assert the contrary.

CHAPTER XV

PRESIDENT: FIRST TERM—
IMPEACHMENTS—REËLECTION

JEFFERSON'S PERSONAL ANIMOSITIES were few. They were limited to the small body of supposed "monocrats," the New England clergy, and the Federalist judges in the courts of the United States. In all his preachings of universal benevolence and political brotherhood there must be understood a tacit reservation against these three classes of the community. Of these the judges presented the most definite mark. It has already been seen how he felt about the exclusive possession of the courts by the Federalists. There is no doubt that he wished, if he could not effect a radical change in the judicial *personnel,* at least to give an impressive lesson to the life-tenants of the benches. His first experiment was certainly made *in corpore vili.* He sent to the Representatives a special message concerning the shortcomings and vices of Pickering of New Hampshire, judge of the District Court, a worthless fellow morally and mentally.* Pickering was at once impeached before the Senate by order of the House, was found guilty and removed, the Federalist senators doing themselves little credit by voting in favor of so wretched a creature.

But this was only light practising; much higher game was aimed at in the person of Judge Chase of Maryland, a justice of the

---

*For modification of the statement concerning Judge Pickering, see *Appendix.*

Supreme Court. He was of unquestioned integrity and ability; but he was a Federalist of the extreme type, and found it as impossible to keep his Federalism out of his charges to juries as Copperfield says that Mr. Dick did to keep King Charles' head out of his memorials. There is no doubt that he erred gravely in this particular, and used his judicial position in a manner improper even in those times, and which in our day would be deemed intolerable. That he was ever led to the commission of an actual injustice does not appear; and whether his offences against official decorum, when they could not be proved ever to have resulted in practical wrong, ought to have been regarded as ground for impeachment was at best doubtful. But Jefferson and his friends resolved to make the trial; in addition to the political advantage which success might bring them, they were incensed against Chase personally, by reason of a speech which he had lately delivered to the grand jury, wherein he had very soundly berated the Democratic party for having repealed the Judiciary Act. However unjustifiable this tirade was, yet it made a narrow foundation for an impeachment. Other charges were therefore sought, and the Republican managers went back nearly five years to the trials of Fries and of Callender, at which Chase had certainly shown his political bias in a manner deserving of reprehension. But these were old stories, and if they were so heinous as was now alleged, at least it followed that the Republicans had been guilty of gross laches in not having long since made them the basis of proceedings for removal. Attaching them to the later causes of complaint constituted a virtual acknowledgment of the insufficiency of these later causes when taken by themselves. Nor was there any object in gathering together many improprieties, all which in conjunction might suffice to show, in a general way, that the judge was unfit for his office. For the question which the Senate must decide was not, whether upon the whole Chase was fit or unfit for his judicial position; but whether upon any one of the specific charges of the impeachment the evidence showed him to be a guilty man.

Jefferson's behavior in this affair was shrewd and selfish. The end which he desired to attain was so desirable that even a small prospect of success justified the endeavor. But a defeat would bring so much condemnation on the losers, and there was so much chance of defeat, that he had no notion of subjecting his own person and fortunes to the risk. Perhaps he felt about his prestige in politics as great generals are entitled to feel about their own lives in battle, that it was too valuable to his party to be jeoparded. Certain it is that he played only the part of an instigator. He did not send in a message, as in the more clear and wholly unimportant case of Pickering. But his faithful henchman, the hot-headed Randolph, equally devoid of caution and of judgment, stood ready at a word from the chief to plunge into any dubious fray. The signal was given to him May 13, 1803, through Nicholas, who was Randolph's personal friend, and acted as his chief of staff in the House of Representatives. To this gentleman Jefferson wrote: "You must have heard of the extraordinary charge of Chase to the grand jury at Baltimore. Ought this seditious and official attack on the principles of our Constitution and on the proceedings of a State to go unpunished? And to whom so pointedly as yourself will the public look for the necessary measures? I ask these questions for your consideration; for myself it is better that I should not interfere." Accordingly to the end he did not interfere; he only watched with profound interest. But he had the disappointment to see the veteran judge, aided by the ablest counsel in the country, prove altogether too much for Randolph. As the cause proceeded, he was compelled to recognize that only the most merciless use of the party whip could dragoon the requisite two thirds of the senators into sustaining the impeachment; and he dared not exert his influence in a cause which it would be so difficult to justify. In silent chagrin he averted his countenance, while Randolph met a severe defeat after a very bitter contest. The administration party was worsted, but its astute leader had been externally so indifferent that he was not compromised in the popular opinion by the blunder of his friends. But he had learned the lesson and made no further attempts to meddle with the bench. It remained to the end an immovable obstacle in the way of the complete triumph of his political theories.

Jefferson's first term in the presidency was a great success. This was not so much due to what he had really done as to what he appeared to have done. For in fact no fundamental changes had been made in the system of administering the national affairs. A different atmosphere prevailed at the capital, but it had affected rather the external aspect than the inner constitution of the government. The work of the Federalist party had not been undone in a single particular of any importance. A certain relaxation was discernible, a certain air of carelessness; but except for the hostility to the army and navy little practical result was observable. All the great constructive measures of that party remained unaltered; the governmental machinery which it had devised was worked by the new hands much as it had been by the old ones. In any matters of substantial importance there was very little more real democracy under the sway of the Democrats, than there had been under that of the Federalists. The democrat Jefferson enjoyed and exercised a personal authority infinitely greater than had been wielded by the "monocrat" Adams. Indeed, even to this day no President since Washington has ever been able to dictate to Congress as Jefferson could do, and upon sufficient occasion actually did. No President since Washington has ever led the people in such unquestioning obedience. But these facts were not clearly recognized at the time. Congress did not appreciate that it was receiving orders; the people had not the slightest notion that they were being guided. For Jefferson never used the accent of command or assumed the bearing of a leader. His influence was singularly shadowy and mysterious. He simply communicated suggestions and opinions to this or that selected one among those who believed in him. The sugges-

tions and opinions were followed not with any consciousness of discipline, but from a true feeling of admiration and confidence towards the great and good statesman who seemed always to speak wisely and to think virtuously; who, at least, had many times been proved to plan with unrivalled astuteness for the good of his party. That party had already begun to abjure the name of Republicans in order to adopt exclusively that of Democrats: the title has ever since been kept, and the identity of the party has been preserved, while its political opponents have had a variety of appellations and have undergone some breaks in continuity, if not some mutations of principle. But it is a singular circumstance that the body which has chosen to declare itself the guardian of democratic principles has always from the outset been peculiarly prone to fall beneath the dictation of a single individual. No leader among the Federalists, the Whigs, or the Republicans (the present party of that name) has ever had a personal supremacy equal to that of Jefferson or that of Andrew Jackson. The Democrats have invariably been most powerful under the sway of a monocrat, and have always taken kindly to that sway.

Jefferson was able from time to time in his first four years to make a very good showing in those matters of detail which were much more definite and obvious than were the generalities of political theories. Thus every one could see that he dressed with ostentatious shabbiness on occasions when dress was likely to be noticed; every one knew that the monarchical levees of Washington and Adams were discontinued. It was also well known that the army had been subjected to such a "chaste reformation" that the smallest remnant only remained. The Federalists allowed no one to forget that the harbors were not properly fortified, and that the navy was not kept up as it should be. Like economies were practised in all other departments. When the odious internal taxes were done away with, and even without them the treasury prospered wonderfully and reduced

the national debt with surprising rapidity, the credit for these
achievements was given to the economy of the administration
and to its able financial management. Really more efficient
causes were the growth and prosperity of the country and the
soundness of the financial policy which Hamilton had inaugu-
rated. But Jefferson would have been more than a Quixote in politics had he frankly admitted that he was only reaping the fields
which Hamilton had sowed. In like manner the freedom from
anxiety about European complications was altogether due to
causes entirely beyond the reach of Jefferson's influence. But fortune had become his friend more than ever before, and everything redounded to his good fame and popularity.* The nation did
not concern itself too critically with the connections of cause and
effect, but feeling very comfortable and good-natured amid the
broad visible facts of the passing time, gave credit for the condition of affairs to the rulers for the time being. Had not Jefferson
always preached economy, and reviled the financial management
of the Federalists; and now were not expenses curtailed, and
taxes reduced, and debts being rapidly diminished? Had not
Jefferson always desired peaceful relations with foreign powers,
and had the country been for many years past so free from irritation and anxiety growing out of foreign affairs? Had not Jefferson
always declared that he sought unity of feeling and the preva-

---

*Jefferson did not hesitate to claim credit for all that he plausibly could. In April, 1802, he
wrote: "The session of the first Congress convened since Republicanism has recovered its
ascendency is now drawing to a close. They will pretty completely fulfil all the desires of the
people. They have reduced the army and navy to what is barely necessary. They are disarm-
ing executive patronage and preponderance by putting down one half the offices of the
United States which are no longer necessary. These economies have enabled them to sup-
press all the internal taxes, and still to make such provisions for the payment of their public
debt as to discharge that in eighteen years. They have lopped off a parasite limb, planted by
their predecessors on their judiciary body for party purposes; they are opening the doors of
hospitality to fugitives from the oppression of other countries; and we have suppressed all
those public forms and ceremonies which tended to familiarize the public eye to the harbin-
gers of another form of government. The people are nearly all united."

lence of universal good-will among the people themselves, and had political kindliness ever before permeated the nation as it did to-day? Four years of prosperity and tranquillity left little room for discontent with the government. Amid such influences political opposition pined and almost died. The Federalist party shrank to insignificant dimensions, indeed, since it flourished chiefly in a narrow locality, and was largely recruited from those peculiar spirits who seem to be by nature malcontents and grumblers, it seemed on the verge of becoming rather a faction than a party.

Such was the condition of affairs when the fifth presidential election took place. At the close of February, 1804, the Republican members of Congress held a caucus and nominated Jefferson as the party candidate for the presidency at the next election. They also very gladly felt that they could safely throw Burr overboard, and they accordingly named George Clinton for the second place. Jefferson could not bring himself to decline a second term. He can hardly be seriously blamed for this, though certainly he became guilty of still another inconsistency which he defended only by so-called reasons which deserved the less honorable name of excuses. His opinion "originally" had been, "that the President of the United States should have been elected for seven years, and be forever ineligible afterwards." But he had "since become sensible that seven years is too long to be irremovable. . . . The service for eight years, with a power to remove at the end of the first four, comes nearer to my principle as corrected by experience." Admirable happiness of expression, that might have planted envy in the breast of the most subtle Jesuit! In adherence to this principle, he adds: "I determine to withdraw at the end of my second term. . . . General Washington set the example of retirement at the end of eight years. I shall follow it; and a few more precedents will oppose the obstacle of habit to any one after a while who shall endeavor to extend his term." So much for his abstract principles. His more specific motives he stated as follows: —

> I sincerely regret that the unbounded calumnies of the
> Federal party have obliged me to throw myself on the
> verdict of my country for trial, my great desire having
> been to retire, at the end of the present term, to a life of
> tranquillity; and it was my decided purpose when I
> entered into office. They force my continuance. If we
> can keep the vessel of state as steadily in her course for
> another four years, my earthly purposes will be accomplished, and I shall be free to enjoy, as you are doing, my
> family, my farm, and my books.

So the Federalists had themselves to thank for the continuance of their much hated opponent in the presidency. They must seek such comfort as they could find in his asseveration that he was very unhappy about it.

A party so large and so omnipotent as the Republicans, or Democrats, had now become, could not long remain wholly free from intestine feuds. Some rifts seemed already to become visible. The followers of Burr were angry at his ignominious displacement; there were dissensions in New York; and symptoms which soon ripened into ill blood were discernible in Pennsylvania. Even the Democrats in the Eastern States were getting much disgusted with the Virginian ascendency. In view of these hopeful facts the Federalists began to cherish schemes of detaching from the main body of Republicans a considerable number of malcontents; then an alliance, in which they would be the more weighty partner, might restore them to power. Jefferson was well aware of these intrigues, but watched them with just contempt. Nothing came of them. When the time arrived, the Republican party in all sections of the country voted solidly and won an overwhelming victory. Even Massachusetts was for once carried by them, to the immense surprise and chagrin of the Federalists. In the electoral colleges one hundred and sixty-two votes were cast for Jefferson and Clinton; fourteen faithful Federalists gave their ballots for C. C. Pinckney and Rufus King. It was a glorious triumph.

CHAPTER XVI

PRESIDENT: SECOND TERM—RANDOLPH'S DEFECTION—BURR'S TREASON

A LONG LIFE of singular good fortune, almost unprecedented in a land of popular government, checkered by few serious and no enduring disappointments, found its culmination in the brilliant victory of the election of 1804. Had Jefferson been as wise as the prince in the fable he would have been alarmed at his own fortune, and have felt reluctant further to test the constancy of his good Genius, knowing how difficult it is to perch long upon the giddy pinnacle of supreme success. Apparently he felt no such boding instinct, but approached his second term with tranquil confidence. This temper was not properly attributable to personal vanity, nor to the overweening ambition which his detractors ascribed to him. Rather it was due to his firm belief that his theories of government were so founded in eternal truth that success and popularity naturally attended upon him as their expositor. So far as he was egotistical and self-confident, he was so because he honestly conceived himself to be a genuine and successful benefactor of mankind. Yet some misgivings and self-distrust would have been more timely, for whatever were his deserts he was about to meet such reverses as experience shows almost inevitably succeed to long continued prosperity.

Not many days after Monroe and Livingston had agreed to purchase Louisiana, war had again broken out in Europe. Nor did hostilities advance far before the ill effects attendant upon all those Napoleonic struggles began to be experienced by the United States, in the too familiar shape of naval outrages and lawless aggressions upon their neutral commerce. Serious complaints were heard, and the outlook was far from cheerful during many months before Jefferson's second inauguration. Yet he obstinately maintained a sanguine temper. Resolved to preserve a fair neutrality, he would not doubt that his just dealing would be reciprocated, and the neutral rights of the United States be respected with moderate honesty. The career in which the French people had sustained Napoleon for many years past had to a great extent cured Jefferson of those Gallican predilections which in Washington's day had given such an unneutral bias to his feelings. Now he had been for some time inclining towards England, not so much with warmth of sentiment as from a respect for her position as the chief obstacle in the way of Bonaparte's military despotism. Even so far back as October, 1802, he had written rather bitterly to Livingston: "It is well, however, to be able to inform you generally . . . that we stand completely corrected of the error that either the government or the nation of France has any remains of friendship for us." In the summer of 1803 he said: "We see . . . with great concern the position in which Great Britain is placed, and should be sincerely afflicted were any disaster to deprive mankind of the benefit of such a bulwark against the torrent which has for some time been bearing down all before it." Again: "We are friendly, cordially and conscientiously friendly, to England. We are not hostile to France. We will be rigorously just and sincerely friendly to both. I do not believe we shall have as much to swallow from them as our predecessors had." In this spirit towards the warring powers, Jefferson felt "a perfect horror at everything like connecting ourselves with the politics of Europe." His wish was that, while the nations of the old world were fighting, the United States should stand by indifferent, or at least impartial, but rapidly amassing riches through the abundant channel of a vast neutral commerce. It was a pleasing and sufficiently honorable project to gather wealth, increase, and power through peace. "The day," he wrote, in one of his happy dreamings, "is within my time as well as yours, when we may say by what laws other nations shall treat us on the sea. And we will say it. In the mean time we wish to let every treaty we have drop off without renewal." It was a civilized policy worthy of respect. Moreover it was a sensible policy. Jefferson alone understood in that time the truth, which is now more generally appreciated, that by sheer growth in population, wealth, and industry a nation gains the highest degree of substantial power and authority.

But Jefferson's attitude was that of a mercantile Quaker seeking an amicable trade with infuriated highwaymen, hardly a feasible attitude to be long maintained. Rage and immediate self-interest alone ruled the combatants, who were about as much influenced by Mr. Jefferson's reasonable and pacific protestations as they were by the Sermon on the Mount. Peace and neutrality were contemptible phrases in their ears. The British cabinet determined that the United States should either become an ally of England or be plundered by English cruisers. France pursued the same policy so far as she could. But Jefferson, resolutely bent upon tranquillity and prosperity, clung to his chosen course, and persisted in protest and negotiation. His expressions of good-will towards England increased. "No two countries upon earth," he said, "have so many points of common interest and friendship, and their rulers must be great bunglers indeed, if, with such dispositions, they break them asunder." It was cruel indeed to have only violence and robbery returned for such resolute amiability. But so it was; and the battle of Trafalgar occurring October 21, 1805, and leaving England supreme upon the ocean, proved a further serious misfortune for the United States, who soon began to suffer more intolerable injuries than any yet inflicted.

Another incident in the first year of his second term gave the

President grave though temporary annoyance. Spain, backed by France, threatened to make serious trouble concerning the eastern boundaries of Louisiana. Jefferson, though irritated and ready to fight if need be, was yet sufficiently true to his principles to prefer the peaceful remedy of a purchase. On December 6, 1805, he sent a private message to the House, with the design that it should lead up to such another appropriation as had been placed at his disposal in the case of Louisiana. But to the surprise and discomfiture of the administrationists, a report of a very different tenor was made by the committee to whom the message was referred; and the chairman of that committee was John Randolph. Here was indeed an alarming defection; for Randolph had long been accustomed to lead the House for the government. He was esteemed daring, able, and influential; and those traits, which later gave him the character of a mere political free lance, had not yet been fully recognized. He had carried through the Louisiana measures with a contempt for logic and law which proved him the best of partisans; he had endured castigation and defeat in the Chase impeachment with a gallantry that made him seem the most loyal of followers. Now suddenly he sprang up on the wrong side and poured forth the most vituperative harangues not only against the policy but even against the political integrity of the President. Jefferson might well be taken aback by this singular behavior, for he had a right to expect the same support in buying the Floridas which had been accorded in buying Louisiana. What then was to be the extent of this scission, this rebellion? For a short time he watched the debates in the House with anxiety. But ere long the votes reassured him; only eleven of the party went off under Randolph's banner; eighty-seven maintained their allegiance to the President. Evidently Randolph's personal influence had been overrated. Not all even of his eleven remained faithful to him, when it appeared that his purpose was not merely a difference upon this single occasion but extended to a permanent opposition. The President took courage, and declared the House to be

> as well disposed as ever I saw one. The defection of so prominent a leader threw them into dismay and confusion for a moment; but they soon rallied to their own principles and let him go off with five or six followers only. . . . The alarm . . . from this schism has produced a rallying together and a harmony, which carelessness and security had begun to endanger. On the whole this little trial of the firmness of our representatives in their principles . . . has added much to my confidence in the stability of our government, and to my conviction that should things go wrong at any time, the people will set them to rights by the peaceable exercise of their elective rights.

Characteristic sentences! Jefferson presents the unusual spectacle of one who grew more optimistic with increasing years.

Yet Randolph's conduct, though of slight political consequence, ought to have given food for reflection to the people. It was not the outgrowth of selfish disappointment, but of a genuine and honest dissatisfaction with the career of the administration. Randolph was really a purist in politics, as Jefferson had professed to be. He had espoused Republicanism and had become the devout disciple of Jefferson because he had believed that absolute purity would prevail beneath the sway of that party and its admirable leader. A Republican triumph was to inaugurate a golden age of virtue. He had been slow to awake from this delusion and to acknowledge that his idol was adopting the ways of all politicians and that the business of government was conducted now much as it had been in the bad days of Federalism. In the pain and anger of disillusionment, the impetuous reformer saw no better course than to abandon a chief whom he chose to regard as forsworn. His criticism was not just, because the critic had set up an ideal standard, and had expected more than could be done. Yet there was a lesson to be learned from his strictures; it was apparent that Jefferson in earlier times had found fault which he had no right to find and raised hopes which he could not fulfil. He had dreamed and promised probably with honesty, but he was not transmuting his dreams into realities nor making his promises good. In truth he could not do so; he had tried, but he had unfortunately talked about impossibilities in government so far as that science had yet been developed.

In 1805–6 another disturbance arose. Aaron Burr had made up his mind that treason was preferable to a condition of political failure. For advancing the purposes of his boundless ambition Burr possessed infinite audacity, a singular capacity for personal fascination, and great aptitude for the machinery of politics. But he needed much weightier qualities to enable him to cope with such powerful leaders as Hamilton and Jefferson, who both, hostile in everything else, were of one mind concerning the necessity of crushing him. Nor did Burr improve matters, but, to his infinite surprise and chagrin, made them vastly worse by the method which he took to rid himself of Hamilton. He only added universal odium to political disaster and financial ruin. In this state of his affairs he concocted his famous scheme for seating himself upon the "throne of the Montezumas," and annexing to it all the territory west of the Alleghanies. While the enterprise was still unchecked and the wildest rumors of its extent and progress were prevalent, Jefferson maintained a tranquil confidence highly creditable to his good sense. He omitted no precaution, but he felt no doubt as to the result. Substantially his anticipations were justified by the prompt and easy shattering of the meagre forces and the arrest of the principal traitor.

When Burr was brought to Richmond for trial, the President took the liveliest interest in the legal proceedings. Then indeed was witnessed a singular spectacle. The Federalists, forgetting that the hands of the criminal were red with the life-blood of that distinguished man to whom their party owed at once its existence and nearly all the measures upon which it could base its good reputation, and seeing in the alleged project of Burr only a scheme which, if successful, would have overwhelmed in disgrace the administration of Jefferson, now received the wretch with every demonstration of friendship and admiration. They pretended to regard him as an innocent man persecuted by the President from motives of personal spite. It is highly improbable that they believed what they said; but even if they did, it ill became them to be upholders of Burr. Accident made it likely that the punishment of a traitor would gratify a private animosity which it may be admitted that the President must have felt, since he was human. But Burr was so unquestionably guilty that Jefferson, as President, was in duty bound to desire his conviction, and it was impossible to say how far personal feeling mingled with public motives. By established rules the President was entitled to the benefit of the doubt. But the Federalists, themselves most shamefully condoning Hamilton's murder, gave their enemy no benefit of any doubt, preferring to pursue him with unbounded abuse.

Jefferson certainly made no secret of his opinion; but there was no reason why he should do so; there was no danger that the naked fact that he thought Burr guilty would have any undue weight in a court over which Marshall was presiding. Indeed, if any influence at all was perceptible in that tribunal, it was the influence of the Federalist friends of the accused. Jefferson, of course, made no effort, as he had no power, to affect the conduct of the trial directly or indirectly, save so far as that he communicated to the government counsel any facts or suggestions which occurred to him. But he watched the proceedings closely, and certainly he had a right to be indignant at some incidents in them. For instance, Luther Martin, himself not untainted by suspicion of collusion with his "highly-respected friend," as he took pains to call Burr in open court, did not hesitate to charge that the President, by "tyrannical orders" "contrary to the Constitution and the laws," had endeavored to consign "to destruction" "the life and property of an innocent man." The judges sat silent while the counsel uttered this and more of the same sort. Then application was made by the defendant's lawyers for a *subpœna duces tecum* to compel the President personally to attend as a witness, bringing the letters and records of the War Department. The court granted the request, but admitted that it had no authority to enforce such a summons. This singular assertion of a right to command not backed by a power to enforce made the President angry. He was ready to send any papers which might be pertinent, but he repudiated the notion that the court could properly order him to take the stand as a witness. There is hardihood, if not professional profanity, in questioning a decision of Marshall; but it certainly seems as though the Federalist rather than the judge spoke on this occasion; and if all his rulings had been as open to criticism and to suspicion as was this one, he might have left a less formidable reputation.

Jefferson wrote to Hay as follows: —

> Laying down the position generally, that all persons owe obedience to subpoenas, he [Marshall] admits no exception unless it can be produced in his law books. . . . The Constitution enjoins his [the President's] constant agency in the concerns of six millions of people. Is the law paramount to this, which calls on him on behalf of a single one? Let us apply the judge's own doctrine to the case of himself and his brethren. The sheriff of Henrico summons him from the bench to quell a riot somewhere in his county. The federal judge is by the general law a part of the posse of the state sheriff. Would the judge abandon major duties to perform lesser ones? Again: the court of Orleans or Maine commands by subpœnas the attendance

of all the judges of the Supreme Court. Would they abandon their posts as judges, and the interests of millions committed to them, to serve the purposes of a single individual? The leading principle of our Constitution is the independence of the Legislature, Executive, and Judiciary of each other; and none are more jealous of this than the Judiciary. But would the Executive be independent of the Judiciary, if he were subject to the commands of the latter, and to imprisonment for disobedience, if the several courts could bandy him from pillar to post, keep him constantly trudging from north to south and east to west, and withdraw him entirely from his constitutional duties?

A striking exemplification of the force of this argument would probably soon have been furnished, had not Burr escaped from a trial in Ohio by forfeiting his bonds and fleeing abroad. For the President would surely have been summoned to that trial also, and, if he had obeyed the summons, would have been kept far from the seat of government, in a then very inaccessible region, at the moment when his presence was of exceptional importance at the capital, by reason of the doings of British cruisers on the Virginian sea-coast, and of the perilous condition of our relations with England. The decision of Marshall was disregarded by the President, and nothing more came of it. Only the Federalists used his conduct as a further support of their accusations of tyranny and injustice.

When the final result was announced Jefferson directed George Hay, of counsel for the government, not to pay or dismiss any witnesses until their testimony should have been taken down in writing. "These whole proceedings," he said, "will be laid before Congress, that they may decide whether the defect has been in the evidence of guilt, or in the law, or in the application of the law, and that they may provide the proper remedy for the past and the future." He was as good as his word, calling the attention of Congress to the matter in his next message in language of unmistakable tenor. The result ultimately was the passage of some useful legislation concerning treason, but, of course, nothing was done in relation to this especial trial, or any individual engaged therein. Matters of greater consequence than the punishment of a ruined man demanded attention.

CHAPTER XVII

PRESIDENT: SECOND TERM—EMBARGO

ANGRY CLOUDS WERE rolling up thick and fast from the Atlantic horizon over the benevolent head of the most pacific of earthly rulers. Jefferson seemed to make a modest and reasonable request of the European powers when he asked only that they would let the United States alone. But it was a request which neither France nor England had any mind to grant. Napoleon would tolerate no neutrality; Great Britain added to her natural vindictiveness towards her quondam colonies a rapacious jealousy of their growing commerce. Her established purpose was to make a double gain at once by confiscation and extermination, and she carried out this policy with brutal insolence, in defiance of international law and natural right. In November, 1804, Jefferson was obliged to admit that even in our own harbors our vessels were no longer safe from British guns. France, though equally ready, was fortunately less able to commit outrages. Yet the President hopefully added: "The friendly conduct of the governments, from whose officers and subjects these acts have proceeded, in other respects and places more under their observation and control, gives us confidence that our representations on this subject will have been properly regarded." A vain hope! A year passed and matters were worse rather than better. In the message of December 3, 1805, Jefferson could say nothing more satisfactory than that

our coasts have been infested and our harbors watched
by private armed vessels, some of them without commissions, some with illegal commissions, others with those
of legal form, but committing piratical acts beyond the
authority of their commissions. They have captured in
the very entrance of our harbors, as well as on the high
seas, not only the vessels of our friends coming to trade
with us, but our own also. They have carried them off
under pretence of legal adjudication; but not daring to
approach a court of justice, they have plundered and
sunk them by the way, or in obscure places where no evidence could arise against them; maltreated the crews
and abandoned them in boats in the open sea or on
desert shores without food or covering.

January 17, 1806, he was further obliged to send in a special
message on the same irritating subject, accompanied by the
"memorials of several bodies of merchants in the United States."
In the subsequent debates a singular alliance was struck between
the Federalists from the commercial districts of New England and
John Randolph, with his half dozen followers,—the "Quids" as
they were called. That there was no real community of interest
between the malcontent planter and the Eastern merchants may
be gathered from Randolph's bold declaration that, "if this great
agricultural nation is to be governed by Salem and Boston, New
York and Philadelphia, and Baltimore and Norfolk and Charleston,
let gentlemen come out and say so." Nevertheless the two bodies
made common cause against the administration. But their strange
coalition was of no avail. The measure desired by the President was
carried by very handsome majorities in both Houses. It provided
that after November 15, 1806, certain articles should not be
imported from the British dominions, nor, if of British manufacture,
from any other places. Mr. Jefferson, still omnipotent, might well

say, "A majority of the Senate means well," and "the House of Representatives is as well disposed as I ever saw one." He believed in mercantile pressure, and he was allowed to have his way.

But his way worked poorly. Less than a month after this act was passed the English war ship Leander fired into an American coaster near Sandy Hook and killed a man. The President ordered the Leander out of American waters, and directed the arrest of her commander, which of course could not conveniently be made. Then, alarmed at the possible effect of this very moderate display of resentment, he wrote to Mr. Monroe, minister at London, deprecating the anger of the newly established and friendly cabinet of Mr. Fog. Public sentiment, he said, "did not permit us to do less than has been done. It ought not to be viewed by the ministry as looking towards them at all, but merely as the consequences of the measures of their predecessors, which their nation has called on them to correct. I hope, therefore, they will come to just arrangements." Obviously Jefferson had forgotten something of what he had once learned concerning the British character, and did not divine the antidotes appropriate to its vices. It has been often said that if he had refrained from his prattle about peace, reason, and right, and instead thereof had hectored and swaggered with a fair show of spirit at this crucial period, the history of the next ten years might have been changed and the war of 1812 might never have been fought. Probably this would not have been the case, and England would have fought in 1807, 1808, or 1809, as readily as in 1812. But however this may be, the high-tempered course was the only one of any promise at all, and had it precipitated the war by a few short years, at least the nation would have escaped a long and weary journey through a mud slough of humiliation. But it is idle to talk of what might have been had Jefferson acted differently. He could not act differently. Though the people would probably have backed him in a warlike policy, he could not adopt it. A great statesman amid political storms, he was utterly helpless when the clouds of war gathered. He was as miserably out of place now as he had been in the governorship of Virginia during the Revolution. He could not bring himself to entertain any measures looking to so much as preparation for serious conflict. A navy remained still, as it had always been, his abhorrence. His extremest step in that direction was to build gunboats. Every one has heard of and nearly every one has laughed at these playhouse flotillas, which were to be kept in sheds out of the sun and rain until the enemy should appear, and were then to be carted down to the water and manned by the neighbors, to encounter, perhaps, the fleets and crews which won the fight at Trafalgar, shattered the French navy at the Nile, and battered Copenhagen to ruins. It almost seemed as though the very harmlessness of the craft constituted a recommendation to Jefferson. At least they were very cheap, and he rejoiced to reckon that nearly a dozen of them could be built for a hundred thousand dollars. So he was always advising to build more, while England, with all her fighting-blood up, inflicted outrage after outrage upon a country whose ruler cherished such singular notions of naval affairs.

Yet Jefferson could vapor a little at times in such a quiet private way as involved no substantial responsibility. He gave vent occasionally to bellicose sentiments concerning Spain, and at some moments was quite ready to fight her about the Louisiana boundaries, or for the Floridas. Once he said: "We begin to broach the idea that we consider the whole Gulf Stream as of our waters, in which hostilities and cruising are to be frowned on for the present, and prohibited so soon as either consent or force will permit us. We shall never permit another privateer to cruise within it, and we shall forbid our harbors to national cruisers. This is essential for our tranquillity and commerce." This grandiloquence occurs in the very letter in which he admits that American ships are fired into, and American sailors are killed with impunity at the very mouths of American harbors. Surely never was man more devoid of a sense of humor!

Meantime, though the British were infesting the Atlantic seaboard like pirates, Jefferson's perfect faith in his own measures and the people's equal confidence in him were unshaken. The Democrats continued to score gains in the elections, until the whole country seemed on the point of becoming solidly of that party. In this state of affairs the Ninth Congress came together on December 1, 1806; and on the next day Jefferson sent in a message in which he said: "The delays . . . in our negotiations with the British government appear to have proceeded from causes which do not forbid the expectation that during the course of the session I may be enabled to lay before you their final issue." Nevertheless a further appropriation for more gunboats was recommended, as matter of course. They were fully as good for peace as for war!

A noteworthy passage in this message, though an episode in the present narrative, deserves a word. It appeared likely that there would soon be a surplus of income over expenditures, and the President said that the use to be made of that surplus demanded consideration.

> Shall we suppress the impost and give that advantage to foreign over domestic manufactures? On a few articles of more general and necessary use the suppression in due season will doubtless be right but the great mass of the articles on which impost is paid is foreign luxuries, purchased by those only who are rich enough to afford themselves the use of them. Their patriotism would certainly prefer its continuance and application to the great purposes of the public education, roads, rivers, canals, and such other objects of public improvement as it may be thought proper to add to the constitutional enumeration of federal powers.

Here was a somersault indeed, which might well confound those who remembered how Republicans had always denounced the theory of internal improvements. It helped the inconsistency not at all that Jefferson admitted the necessity of a constitutional amendment in order to render lawful the expenditures which he contemplated. For his party had maintained not only that such projects were, but also that they ought to be, unconstitutional. Yet now Jefferson, who had preached that the Union was and ought to remain a league for the sole purpose of foreign relationships, that the States were and ought to remain supreme and independent governments in respect of all internal and domestic affairs,—Jefferson was actually urging this doctrine of internal improvements, on the very alleged ground that it would unify, nationalize, centralize the people and the government! "By these operations," he said, "new channels of communication will be opened between the States; *the lines of separation will disappear*, their interests will be identified; and their union cemented by new and indissoluble ties." Hamilton would have had some entertaining comments for this extraordinary politico-economical conversion to his principles.

To return to foreign affairs: on December 3, 1806, the President sent in a special message advising the "further suspension" of the Non-Importation Act which had not yet been put in force. His motive was that Mr. Fox had become prime minister and was supposed to cherish friendly sentiments towards the United States. The obedient majority did his bidding, encountering only a trifling opposition from the Federalists. February 19, 1807, the President announced that Monroe and Pinckney had at last succeeded in coming to terms with Great Britain; though unfortunately the pleasure of the news was seriously dashed by rumors that impressment was not disposed of. Within a few days this disappointment was made certain by the receipt of the treaty, showing that the negotiators had followed the example of Mr. Jay in taking the best they could get rather than nothing. But this best seemed to Jefferson so bad that he would not for a moment consider it. Loath to fight for the national rights, at least he would not compromise them even by remote inference. In negotiation he had infinite courage and obstinacy. Accordingly, without communicating the treaty to the Senate, though that body was then in session, he at once returned it to Monroe, stating that it would not do at all, and that negotiations should be resumed for a widely different conclusion. No one could find fault with his opinion concerning the treaty, but the Federalists assailed the manner of the rejection as high-handed and autocratic. It had this character rather in appearance than in substance; yet such an act done by John Adams would not have escaped Jefferson's bitter animadversion.

Though Jefferson sent back the treaty, he took care, at the same time, to manifest his still pacific temper by exercising the discretionary power which Congress had vested in him further to suspend the Non-Importation Act. Unfortunately a Christian and commercial disposition was hopelessly out of tune with the times. The English policy was simple: since the Americans would not fight, they were the easier objects of plunder. The French principle was responsive: since the Americans are to be robbed, we must share in the booty. So from time to time came British Orders in Council, and retaliatory French decrees dated by the victorious Bonaparte from the conquered capitals, Berlin and Milan. The ultimate result of all these taken together was, that substantially nothing but their own coasting trade was left open to American vessels. One half the mercantile world was sealed up by the British; the other half by the French. Ships not complying with certain regulations were liable to capture by English cruisers; ships complying with those regulations were subject to seizure by French vessels; and vice versa. Nor could even the trade betwixt their own ports be carried on by the citizens of the United States with safety, for British vessels prowled even in our home waters in search of seamen, and in a few years carried off thousands of victims. Their audacity was even such that in June, 1807, the English warship Leopard actually fired a broadside into the American frigate

Chesapeake, just outside Hampton Roads, killing and wounding several men. The Chesapeake, not prepared for action, struck her colors; the British commander boarded her and carried off four sailors, American citizens, three of them at least being native born. One of them was forthwith hanged at Halifax.

The news of this outrage threw the nation into a great rage. "Never," said Jefferson, "since the battle of Lexington, have I seen this country in such a state of exasperation as at present." Some among the extreme Federalists of the New England States, terrified at the prospect of hostilities with England, justified the English commander; but most of the party were too high-spirited for such conduct, and joined in the indignant outcry of the Republicans. "The Federalists themselves coalesce with us as to the object, although they will return to their old trade of condemning every step we take towards obtaining it," said Jefferson. He himself was deeply incensed, but acknowledged the obligation to take no irrevocable step in the heat of passion. "Duty," he considered, "requires that we do no act which shall commit Congress in their choice between war, non-intercourse, and other measures." But he at once dispatched a vessel to England to demand reparation, and summoned Congress to meet in special session on October 26, by which time he hoped to have a reply. "Reason," he said, "and the usage of civilized nations require that we should give them an opportunity of disavowal and reparation. Our own interest, too, the very means of making war, requires that we should give time to our merchants to gather in their vessels and property and our seamen now afloat." It is plain that at this time he anticipated war. He declared that he was making "every preparation" for it "which is within our power," and possibly he really thought that he was getting the country into warlike shape. But he was pitifully mistaken. He only got out some gunboats, did some trifling work on harbor fortifications, and gathered a small amount of supplies. Congress afterward made some petty appropriations to pay for these things.

On October 26, 1807, Congress came together. In both Houses a majority, even more overwhelming than ever before, consisted of administrationists, a term quite as properly to be used in describing them as either Republicans or Democrats, for they were thoroughly subject to the personal influence of Jefferson. It was evident that whatever measures he should recommend would be promptly carried. Yet he was content in his message only to communicate the state of affairs, which was already well known, and to let the development of his policy await the English reply concerning the Chesapeake outrage. This reply did not arrive until the second week in December, and then it was only learned that England would send a special envoy about the matter.

A few days later, on December 18, Mr. Jefferson sent in a brief but momentous message. The communications accompanying it, he said, would show "the great and increasing dangers with which our vessels, our seamen, and merchandise are threatened on the high seas and elsewhere from the belligerent powers of Europe, and it being of great importance to keep in safety these essential resources, I deem it my duty to recommend the subject to the consideration of Congress, who will doubtless perceive all the advantages which may be expected from an inhibition of the departure of our vessels from the ports of the United States." It was afterwards made a serious question whether or not, at the time of sending this message, the President had information of the British Orders in Council dated November 11, held back from formal issuance until November 17, declaring a "paper blockade" of all the ports of France and her allies. The English ministry and their friends, the American Federalists, always maintained that Jefferson had no proper knowledge of these Orders, and that his recommendation of an embargo was a premature and unjustifiable act of unfriendliness. The administrationists retorted that Jefferson had the intelligence, though not in official form. Really the point, if it could be made good, deserved to be disregarded, and could have been preferred only by the immeasurable insolence of Mr. Canning. The communication would have been formally made if England had not behaved with shameful disingenuousness. She pretended to send Mr. Rose as a special emissary in the Chesapeake affair, but, besides hampering him with such preposterous conditions that he could only disclose them and sail home again, she also held back these Orders in Council, until literally a few hours after his departure from London. The honorable motive was that the United States might receive and treat with him in ignorance of them. It hardly became a minister, guilty of such sharp practice, to complain that Mr. Jefferson had been a little too ready with a demonstration of unfriendliness.

So now at last the presidential policy was announced,—not war, but commercial pressure, an embargo. The history of the brief remnant of Mr. Jefferson's administration is little else than a narrative of Federalist attacks on this measure, and its defence by the administrationists. At first it was surprisingly popular. In the Senate John Quincy Adams not only deserted his party in order to vote for it, but said: "The President has recommended this measure on his high responsibility. I would not consider, I would not deliberate, I would act. Doubtless the President possesses such further information as will justify the measure." The senators accepted this reason and this suggestion. Jefferson advised; deliberation was superfluous. In a session of only four hours, behind closed doors, under a suspension of the rules, the bill was passed on the same day on which the message was received. In the House the Federalists kept up a debate for three days, but also with closed doors. Except for this brief delay they were powerless, and the bill was carried by 82 to 44. The vote, however, showed that some few Republicans had for once gone over to the Federalists and the "Quids."

It has been pretty generally agreed in subsequent times that the embargo was a blunder. Certainly the world has outgrown such measures just as it has outgrown Jefferson's amphibious gunboats.

It is hard to realize that only three quarters of a century ago neither of these ideas, more especially that of the embargo, had become discredited. On the contrary, in 1807–8 an embargo was a reputable measure of statecraft, supposed to be efficient both defensively and offensively. In the United States especially the people had been wont for more than a generation to regard it with peculiar favor. So now the policy was hailed with approbation by an overwhelming majority. Some Federalist newspapers had cried out for it; and even many of the most influential merchants were strongly in favor of it, though possibly from the interested motive of wearing out their poorer competitors. Moreover, it was supposed by all that this embargo, like earlier ones, would be of reasonably short duration; and though the Federalists called attention to the fact that the present act, unlike its predecessors, did not establish any limit of time, yet few persons honestly feared that this omission had any dangerous significance.

Jefferson argued very fairly that we should save the property of our citizens, and the persons of our sailors, by keeping our ships in our own harbors, whereas on the high seas both merchandise and men would be stolen. The device did not seem to him ignoble. Moreover, since commerce was to be forbidden in foreign no less than in domestic bottoms, he was able to depict great numbers of British merchants suffering loss and ruin, and throngs of British artificers reduced to starvation by the consequent curtailment of industry. English laborers, he said, could not, like Americans, readily adopt new occupations; neither had they that surplus of food which our farmers enjoyed. He spoke as if all Americans were farmers; and gave no thought to the great seaboard population wholly dependent upon trade. If they were to be hurt, he at least expected them to be kept silent by patriotism, while he anticipated that the clamors of the English malcontents would overawe Parliament and the administration. A certain amount of sound reason which really lay in these arguments, backed by the confident assent of a vast majority of the nation, and soon corroborated by cheering accounts from Mr. Pinckney concerning the effect of the pressure in England, constituted perhaps a justification for Mr. Jefferson in the outset. But in order to make this justification complete two things were necessary, both obviously implied in the reasoning of the administrationists. First: so far as the embargo was a domestic measure, *i.e.* designed to save our ships and sailors, it should obviously be accompanied by vigorous preparations for war, since it was absurd to regard an embargo as a permanently saving device; before long it would constitute destruction; it could only be used to save until the other means to that end customary among nations could be resorted to. Secondly: so far as the embargo had a foreign aspect, *i.e.* was designed to influence British legislation, it was properly experimental only, and so soon as the working of the experiment clearly promised failure, it should have been abandoned.

Now in point of fact it was impossible long to defend the measure in the former of these two aspects, because the lapse of time showed no serious purpose to protect by sufficient force the men and property subjected to the embargo. To save them by shutting them up until preparation could be made to protect them when abroad was therefore clearly not the government policy. Hence the measure, if it was to be defended at all after the passing of a few months, must be defended in its second or foreign character. But here, unfortunately, it was utterly and hopelessly indefensible. The clamor had been raised, and the British government had turned a deaf ear to it, for reasons altogether too attractive to be readily rejected. The merchants who were injured by the cessation of the American trade would probably suffer only temporarily; at any rate they were only individual victims of a great national policy, destined to work an immense and lasting benefit to the entire shipping and mercantile interests of their country. It was the established aim of the English government to annihilate American commerce, which already threatened a dangerous rivalry with their own. In ministerial eyes the embargo was a welcome and efficient aid, blindly furnished by their competitor against itself. Jefferson ought to have understood this, and appreciated that England could play at his game longer and with much more profit than the United States. For while in England a few suffered, in the United States the whole vast industries of shipping and commerce were subjected to a process of starvation which in time would result in utter destruction. The longer the United States endured, the more they advanced the English scheme. That scheme was a permanent policy, whereas the United States were seeking only an immediate, specific object, namely, a recognition of their rights without enforcement by war. Failing in this, as ultimately they did fail in it, they were wholly losers. Even succeeding in it, they would sustain a serious injury, because they would return much weakened to a sharp competition. Whereas in any possible event the English must gain considerably; for every set-back encountered by American commerce was a positive advancement of English commerce.

It may be further remarked that if the embargo accomplished nothing as against England, neither did it do better as against France. That country, herself little hurt by the embargo, was satisfied to have it continue in force. For the permanent commercial ambition of England disturbed Napoleon very little. He was content to see that for the immediate present his foe was cut off from supplies, and subjected to a partial impoverishment.

Unfortunately the English policy was by no means intrinsically devoid of shrewdness or efficiency. The discouragement which American merchants endured for many years prior to the war of 1812, followed by the dangers and losses encountered during that war, constituted the first and powerful influence operating to destroy American commerce. Had the mercantile and shipping interests not been weakened by the prolonged emaciation inflicted by the home government, they might have remained sufficiently powerful to keep within reasonable limits that ill-advised legislation which has since completed the destruction initiated by Jefferson's measures. Unintentionally he, who many years before had expressed his antipathy to commerce, now did it an injury from which it never recovered. But it was through sheer ignorance, not in malice.

As Jefferson did not see that he was serving the merchants very ill, so he would not admit that he was being false to his own principles. The Federalists said that no such example of "strong government" had ever been seen while they were in power. Their embargoes had been brief and simple affairs in comparison with this unlimited and monstrous one. But they were talking of what was really matter of discretion rather than of principle; for if an embargo was a lawful measure, its duration in any especial case was to be determined by a judgment upon the exigencies of that case. The argument that, because the act creating this embargo did not specify its length, therefore it did not "regulate" but destroyed commerce, and was unconstitutional, was very properly overruled by the Supreme Court. But Jefferson was not true to his principles, because, of his two reasons, one at least was thoroughly undemocratic. The endeavor to take care of the property and persons of American citizens by shutting them up, as it were, within doors was the extremity of paternal government. It might have borne a different character had it been a war measure, but within a very short time every one knew that it was not a war measure, but simply an act of paternity. Jefferson constantly spoke of it in this light. As such it was not only undemocratic, but eminently foolish. Jefferson might wisely have left to the merchants the care both of their profits and of their principal. They were not a stupid or a helpless class, and they understood their business far better than he did. The argument was advanced by Quincy of Massachusetts; it could not be answered, but it was disregarded.

Thus it appears that when, through Jefferson's influence, the embargo was imposed it was not to be regarded as absolutely a sound and wise measure. It required to be vindicated either by the doing of certain things in the United States, or the occurrence of certain events in England. After a reasonable time those things had not been done at home and those events had not taken place abroad. For the latter, Jefferson was not responsible; for the former, he was. For he had but to say the word to Congress and he would have been strictly obeyed. He was so supreme and so well known to be a strong advocate of peace, that had he asserted the necessity of creating a navy and building fortifications, or even beginning hostilities, these steps would have been taken at once.

Jefferson's biographers narrate with pleasure the at first enthusiastic and afterward patient support which Congress and the people yielded to the embargo policy, as if this constituted his justification. But the argument is unsatisfactory. It was Jefferson's function to be wiser than the people, to guide and instruct them; or at least he assumed this duty. Congress and the nation persevered in the embargo for the same reason that they had enacted and applauded it in the first instance; and that reason had been forcibly and clearly expressed in Mr. Adams' statement that his reliance was upon the "President's responsibility." Such also was the reliance of the embargo majorities in and out of Congress. Jefferson at first invited and afterward encouraged this faith. It was not until after the miscarriage and unpopularity of the measure had become unquestionable that he began to find his "responsibility" irksome and to seek to shift it from his wearied shoulders. One thing, however, it is fair to say: when an administration blunders it usually receives sound instruction from the opposition; Jefferson did not. The Federalists were even blinder than the administrationists. They showed their ignorance of the true bearing of the embargo by their criticisms upon it. Their horizon also was bounded by the immediate injury to Great Britain, and they stigmatized the measure as a "sly and cunning" endeavor to render surreptitious aid to France. They were even more opposed to warlike measures than

were the Democrats, and had no better advice to give than an ignominious submission to all English demands.

The embargo message, it will be remembered, was sent in to
Congress on December 18, 1807. On March 23, 1808, Jefferson
wrote to Levi Lincoln of Massachusetts, that "it appears to be
approved, even by the Federalists of every quarter except yours.
The alternative was between that and war, and in fact it is the last
card we have to play short of war." By June 23, 1808, he wrote, "the
day is not distant when that [war] will be preferable to a longer continuance of the embargo." By August 9, we get glimpses of serious
popular discontent. On that day the President writes to the
Secretary of War, in language wonderfully different from that
which he had held at the time of the whiskey insurrection, and
with a spirit that would have been better displayed towards trans-
Atlantic enemies than towards suffering American citizens: —

> The Tories of Boston openly threaten insurrection if
> their importation of flour is stopped. The next post will
> stop it. I fear your Governor is not up to the tone of these
> parricides, and I hope, on the first symptom of an open
> opposition of the law by force, you will fly to the scene
> and aid in suppressing any commotion.

Jefferson was neither awed nor instructed by the loud grum-
bling in New England. The day which in March he had described
as "not distant" gave little promise of drawing nearer. To the
marine interest it seemed to be mysteriously established in a perpetual offing; it became in time as exasperating as a mirage.

By September, 1808, Jefferson had become hopeless of affect-
ing the policy of England by longer persistence in the embargo. Mr.
Pinckney, he said, inferred from a conversation with Canning that
the orders might be repealed: "but I have little faith in diplomatic
inferences and less in Canning's good faith." Still the time glided
on until Congress met on November 7. The whole country waited

anxiously to hear what Jefferson would say to that body; would he declare that "not distant" day to be at length near at hand? would the disappointment abroad, the discontent at home, and later the loss by his party of all the New England States save one at the Presidential election, have any weight with him? His message was non-committal. He stated that he had intimated to England that a withdrawal of her Orders in Council would be met by a suspension of the embargo as to her, whatever might be the action of France; but he admitted that the English cabinet had paid no attention to this communication. In a word, he acknowledged that his "candid and liberal experiment" had "failed," and said that now it must "rest with the wisdom of Congress to decide on the course best adapted" to the existing state of affairs. Apparently he meant to give no more advice and to take no more responsibility. He plumed himself a little because the embargo had "demonstrated to foreign nations the moderation and firmness which govern our councils." But he did not add that Great Britain had watched with exasperating complacency this patient endurance with which the United States had suffered for her benefit. Neither did he mention that when our minister had made to Mr. Canning the offer to repeal the embargo if England would repeal the Orders, that sarcastic gentleman had replied that he should like to help the Americans to get rid of the restrictions which they found so very "inconvenient," though he really could not go so far as to withdraw his Orders for that purpose. Bonaparte also, with practical irony, had issued a decree for the seizure of all American ships found afloat, out of friendship, he said, to the United States, to aid them in preventing the escape of their vessels in contravention of their law. Jefferson, having no humor in his composition, did not amuse Congress by repeating these remarks.

By refraining from uttering a word pointing towards war, Jefferson made it plain enough that he did not desire it. The embargo, from being a temporary measure, was beginning to be embraced by him as a policy of indefinite duration. The result was a surprising indication of his almost despotic supremacy. An enormous majority in the House of Representatives adopted a series of resolutions indorsing the continuance of the embargo. In the Senate a direct resolution to repeal it received only six yeas against twenty-five nays; and on December 21 that body passed a very strong enforcing bill. But it was not long before the President and administrationists got alarming evidence of their folly. The Massachusetts Legislature condemned the enforcing bill as "unjust, oppressive, and unconstitutional, and not legally binding." Governor Trumbull of Connecticut refused to comply with the President's requisition for militia under the new act, and sent to the Legislature a message breathing the spirit of nullification. That body, in response, passed resolutions similar to those of Massachusetts. Evasions of the law were countenanced by public opinion, and convictions could not be got before juries. Many influential Federalists began to accustom their minds to the idea of secession, if not actually to form definite plans for it. Of this menacing temper Jefferson received information. Whether or not it frightened him is doubtful. His conduct henceforth becomes so wavering that his true sentiments cannot be accurately ascertained. In November, 1808, he did not desire a repeal. On January 14, 1809, he said that the objects which the embargo was originally designed to subserve were nearly attained, so that the measure was "now near its term." A few days afterward a bill was passed for an extra session of Congress in May next, with the design of repealing the embargo on June 1, and "then resuming and maintaining by force our right of navigation." This apparently ought to have pleased Jefferson, if he clung to his opinion of January 14; but it did not. He still hugged the vision of peace with painful tenacity, and treated the policy of hostility as men treat old age, pushing it always a little in advance of the present day. He moaned somewhat, because the exceptional "situation of the world," such as he declared never had been before and probably never would be again, had defeated his fair policy. "If we go to war now," he complained, "I fear we may renounce forever the hope of seeing an end of our national debt. If we can keep at peace eight years longer, our income, liberated from debt, will be adequate to any war, without new taxes or loans, and our position and increasing strength will put us *hors d'insulte* from any nation." Yet it was his friend and the leader of the administrationists in the House, Nicholas of Virginia, who, on January 25, introduced resolutions contemplating a repeal of the embargo on June 1. An eager debate upon these resulted in a breaking up and reorganizing of parties and cliques which was quite kaleidoscopic. The date was finally set at March 4. This vote was regarded as a defeat of the administration, but only in so far as it made the date of repeal earlier than the contemplated date of May 1 by nearly three months—not a serious period. Yet eighteen months later, partly probably in reference to this vote, and partly to subsequent votes of a like tenor, Jefferson wrote: "The Federalists during their short-lived ascendency have nevertheless, by forcing from us the repeal of the embargo, inflicted a wound on our interests which can never be cured." It looks very much as though the President did not know his own mind; if he did, certainly he succeeded in preventing posterity from finding it out. The truth is that he knew his policy to have failed, yet could not abandon it. He seems to have been bitterly disappointed, and a little frightened. He was pained to see his party defeated, but his chief anxiety was becoming personal, centring in the desire to escape from his embarrassing position. He had not longed more to get out of the governorship of Virginia than he now longed to get out of the presidency. At times he resolved not to try to make up his mind, not to do or advise anything. Even in December, 1808, he said: "I have thought it right to take no part myself in proposing measures, the execution of which will devolve on my successor. I am, therefore, chiefly an unmeddling listener to what others say." In other words he renounced the duty of governing the country for nearly three months before he was lawfully relieved from it. Toward the close of January he reiterated, "I am now so near retiring that I take no part in affairs beyond the expression of an opinion. I think it fair that my successor should now originate those measures, of which he will be charged with the execution and responsibility. . . . Five weeks more will relieve me from a drudgery to which I am no longer equal."

These protestations may be believed. Jefferson appears in no degree responsible for the subsequent action of Congress in curtailing the duration of that measure which had originally been his own. On March 4, 1809, he was probably almost as glad to leave the presidency as eight years before he had been to enter it. He was released from disappointment, from failure, and from imminent humiliation. During the closing months of his administration he had presented a pitiable spectacle of a ruler helplessly confounded by the miscarriage of a policy. Yet his personal prestige, though diminished, was still immense. Probably three quarters of the nation believed him the greatest, wisest, and most virtuous of living statesmen. He had the rare pleasure of transmitting the government to a successor over whom his personal influence was very great, who was in thorough political sympathy with him, and towards whom he succeeded in maintaining a personal friendliness without example in the history of the country. He had even to a considerable extent enjoyed the rare privilege of naming that successor. It is true that Madison was pointed out for the place by his official position, his eminent services, and his abundant ability; yet at one time a strong effort was made to set up Monroe as a competitor. The movement made a brief show of becoming formidable. Jefferson avowed that he would take no sides as between two men, each of whom he loved and trusted. But Monroe entertained uncomfortable suspicions, which were fostered by the malicious communications of persons professing to be friends to him, and who certainly were enemies of the President. A slight coolness ensued in spite of Jefferson's protestations; but it did not last long. Jefferson was the most conciliatory of men, and Monroe had really no choice but to be pacified. Jefferson probably told the truth when he said that he took no part for either competitor. There is no evidence that he was in any way active in Madison's behalf. On the other hand, it cannot be denied that Madison had long before been designed by him for the position, that this was perfectly well understood, and that the knowledge of his wishes was conclusive.

Jefferson had been earnestly besought by many and influential bodies of citizens to become a candidate for a third term. Probably he could have had the honor, had he sought it. But he declined promptly and without the least wavering. He had already stretched his avowed principles concerning the duration of incumbency quite far enough; neither could he now add anything to a fame so great that it could be increased more by declining than by accepting further distinctions. Moreover the times began to look stormy and uncomfortable. He would be sixty-five years old at the close of his second term; he had been in public life, with trifling interruptions, for about forty years; he had enjoyed an amount and constancy of good fortune rare in any polity and almost unprecedented in a republic. He retired with a reputation and popularity hardly inferior to that of Washington. He could dictate the foreign and domestic policy of seven millions of free and critical people, simply by virtue of the personal confidence reposed in his integrity and judgment. It is difficult to suggest any other example parallel to this. No personal influence of a civilian, not nourished in any degree by successful war, has ever been so great and so permanent over our people. In a fair measure this was deservedly the case, for with all his faults Jefferson had very civilized ideas and was the true friend of the commonalty. While he regarded their welfare as the noblest object of government, he did not confer benefits upon them as boons, like a political charity done by superiors to inferiors. He believed in them; he esteemed their intelligence; he not only respected their power, but he desired to see them use it, because he was firmly convinced that they would use it well. He was called a demagogue, but he was not, if that word indicates disingenuousness in preaching popular doctrines. Jefferson had a profound and honest faith in his avowed principles, expecting indeed to gain by them, but only because he thought they were fundamentally right and therefore sure in time to prevail. He differed from the time-serving politician, because he staked his individual success upon the success of what he deemed intrinsically right principles. He differed even from the statesman who acts conscientiously upon every measure, inasmuch as, beyond devising specific measures, he set forth a broad faith or religion in statesmanship, making special measures only single blocks in the wide pavement of his road. He was sometimes insincere, often inconsistent, generally prone to shun hurt and danger to himself; but from the time when he began his great reforms in the Virginia House of Burgesses, the general tendency and large lines of his purposes and policy held with much steadiness in the noble direction of a perfect humanitarianism. To this day the multitude cherish and revere his memory, and in so doing pay a just debt of gratitude to a friend who not only served them, as many have done, but who honored and respected them, as very few have done.

CHAPTER XVIII

AT MONTICELLO: POLITICAL OPINIONS

JEFFERSON'S INTEREST IN public affairs had become a part of his nature and could not suddenly cease. Accordingly in his retirement he corresponded constantly with the new President, exercising an authority in the Republican party not altogether unlike that which had been exercised by Hamilton, in private life, over the Federalists. But in time this relationship caused fault-finding, and gave rise to disagreeable insinuations that Madison was only the puppet of the ex-President. Of course Madison was no man's puppet, but such language was so fitted to wound his feelings and weaken his prestige that Jefferson, from a sense of delicacy, thereafterward greatly curtailed his communications.

A few of Jefferson's opinions on public affairs deserve to be noted. He anticipated for the new administration a peaceful and prosperous career. War, indeed, still hovered in his view as a possibly "less losing business than unrestricted depredation;" but in his desire to avoid it he advised, in the "present maniac state of Europe," not to "estimate the point of honor by the ordinary scale." Yet he was against making permanent concessions of principle; and when a commercial treaty was in prospect he urged Madison not to allow the English to "whip us into a treaty" as "they did in Jay's case and were near doing in Monroe's."

He indulged in a wonderful vision of territorial aggrandizement. Bonaparte, he said, would give us the Floridas to withhold intercourse with the residue of those [the Spanish] colonies. But that is no price; because they are ours in the first moment of the first war; and until a war they are of no particular necessity to us. But, although with difficulty, he will consent to our receiving Cuba into our Union. . . . That would be a price, and I would immediately erect a column on the southernmost limit of Cuba and inscribe on it *ne plus ultra* as to us in that direction. We should then have only to include the North in our confederacy, which would be of course in the first war, and we should have such an empire for liberty as she has never surveyed since the creation; and I am persuaded no constitution was ever before so well calculated as ours for extensive empire and self-government.

In 1809 this was tolerably gorgeous daydreaming!

He had by this time so far modified his old hostility to commerce and manufactures as to say: "An equilibrium of agriculture, manufactures and commerce is certainly become essential to our independence. Manufactures sufficient for our consumption, of what we raise the raw material, (and no more); commerce sufficient to carry the surplus produce of agriculture beyond our own consumption, to a market for exchanging it for articles we cannot raise, (and no more)."

He wrote to Gallatin urging him to be persistent in extinguishing the national debt. "The discharge of the debt," he said, "is vital to the destinies of our government, and it hangs on Mr. Madison and yourself alone. . . . I had always cherished the idea that you would fix on that object the measure of your fame and of the gratitude which our country will owe you." He had a warm regard for Gallatin, and when in the winter of 1810–11 attacks were made on the Secretary, and seams began to open in the party, Jefferson exerted all his authority to stay the disagreement. He preached conciliation eloquently, and laid down a rule of adherence to party which expressed happily the middle course between excessive individual independence and a sacrifice of conscientious opinion.

In the spring of 1812 Jefferson saw that war was imminent. "Our two countries," he wrote to an English friend, "are to be at war, but not you and I. And why should our two countries be at war when by peace we can be so much more useful to one another? Surely the world will acquit our government from having sought it. Never before has there been an instance of a nation bearing so much as we have borne." This was true enough; Jefferson and Madison had carried endurance far past the praiseworthy limit; they were not accountable for the blood-letting to come.

Jefferson contemplated in his usual sanguine temper a war which turned out so very disastrously. He modestly hoped that we should confine ourselves to the defence of our harbors and to the conquest of the British possessions in North America! "The acquisition of Canada," he said, "this year, as far as the neighborhood of Quebec, would be a mere matter of marching, and would give us experience for the attack of Halifax the next, and the final expulsion of England from the American continent." Of course he showed his native incapacity for military affairs. "The partisans of England here," he said, "have endeavored much to goad us into the folly of choosing the ocean instead of the land for the theatre of war. That would be to meet their strength with our own weakness, instead of their weakness with our strength." Quite the reverse of this proved to be the case. Strange as it may seem, he was "importuned from several quarters to become a candidate for the presidency in 1812." So blind was the admiration of his partisans! Further, Mr. Randall also tells us, "on the authority of an intimate friend of Mr. Madison, who heard the fact from his own lips," that Madison offered the position of Secretary of State to Jefferson. Upon this subject Jefferson wrote to Duane, October 1, 1812: "I profess so much of the Roman principle as to deem it honorable for the general of yesterday to act as a corporal to-day, if his services can be useful to his country; holding that to be false pride which postpones the public good to any private or personal considerations. But I am past service. The hand of age is upon me. The decay of bodily faculties apprises me that those of the mind cannot but be impaired." He continues in this melancholy strain, and concludes by expressing his satisfaction that he "retains understanding enough to be sensible how much of it he has lost and to avoid exposing himself as a spectacle for the pity of his friends; that he has surmounted the difficult point of knowing when to retire." This might have been an excuse, but probably was not; for he was now constantly harping upon the failure of his faculties.

He was glad finally to have peace concluded; he hoped that, "having spared the pride of England her formal acknowledgment of the atrocity of impressments, . . . she will concur in a convention for relinquishing it." Otherwise the pacification could be nothing more than a "*truce*, determinable on the first act of impressment of an American citizen." He deprecated "the maniac course of hostility and hatred" pursued by England toward the United States.

> I hope in God she will change. There is not a nation on the globe with whom I have more earnestly wished a friendly intercourse on equal conditions. . . . I know that their creatures represent me as personally an enemy to England. But fools only can believe this, or those who think me a fool. I am an enemy to her insults and injuries. I am an enemy to the flagitious principles of her administration, and to those which govern her conduct towards other nations. But would she give to morality some place in her political code, and especially would she exercise decency and, at least, neutral passions

> towards us, there is not, I repeat it, a people on earth
> with whom I would sacrifice so much to be in friendship.

Certainly no man was ever less prone to nourish a feud than was Jefferson. He always wanted to conciliate, to forgive, to restore lost or shattered friendships. About this time he made up his old quarrel with John Adams, and was corresponding with him most cordially. This is only one of many instances of an attractive trait in his character, giving a most amiable notion of him,—yet he left behind him those venomous "Anas," among the most unfortunate of all deeds of the pen. Beneath an universal good-will it is shocking to find rankling a vindictiveness so relentless and so ignobly indulged. How differently could we think of him were it not for this bequest which, like the cloven foot, peeps out from beneath his apparent guise of broad charity and kindliness.

In 1820 he was profoundly disturbed by the Missouri Compromise, which seemed to him pregnant with a brood of terrible retributive disasters.

"This momentous question," he said, "like a firebell in the night, awakened and filled me with terror. I considered it at once as the knell of the Union. It is hushed, indeed, for the moment. But this is a reprieve only, not a final sentence." "The coincidence of a marked principle, moral and political, with a geographical line, once conceived, I feared would never more be obliterated from the mind; that it would be recurring on every occasion, and renewing irritations until it would kindle such mutual and mortal hatred as to render separation preferable to eternal discord."

He foresaw civil war. "Are we then to see again Athenian and Lacedæmonian confederacies? To wage another Peloponnesian war?" Yet though he was thus correctly prescient of the awful future, he was sadly blind alike to the character and to the result of the conflicts. "It is not," he said, "a moral question, but one merely of power. Its object is to raise a geographical principle for the choice of a President, and the noise will be kept up till that is effected." The moral element was still far beneath the surface, and common men might not have suspected its existence; but Jefferson should have done so. He was not more excusable when he anticipated that the North would be the section to suffer most from the schism. The Northerners, he predicted, "will find the line of separation very different from their 36° of latitude, and as manufacturing and navigating States they will have quarrelled with their bread and butter; and I fear not that after a little trial they will think better of it, and return to the embraces of their natural and best friends." Such is prophecy in statesmanship.

Further, he was decidedly of the opinion that in the compromise Congress interfered unjustifiably with states' rights. He condemned the endeavor "to regulate the condition of the different descriptions of men composing a State. This certainly is the exclusive right of every State, which nothing in the Constitution has taken from them and given to the general government." His views concerning emancipation had apparently undergone little change since the early days when he had concocted a scheme for it, except that apparently he gave greater weight now than previously to the practical difficulties. "The cession of that kind of property [slaves], for so it is misnamed, is a bagatelle which would not cost me a second thought, if in that way a general emancipation and *expatriation* could be effected; and gradually and with due care, I think, it might be. But as it is we have the wolf by the ears, and can neither hold him nor safely let him go."

In 1821 Jefferson had a sharp revival of his old jealousy of the judiciary, and published some letters on the subject. Later, during the administration of J. Q. Adams, he was also greatly annoyed by the complete victory of the policy of internal improvement. He now gave up this battle as hopelessly lost to his side. "The torrent of general opinion" he recognized as "irresistible." He was very mournful about it. He could not reconcile himself to a liberal construction which seemed to him a perversion of the Constitution, no matter how great advantages could be gained thereby. Apparently he was also much less tolerant of the principle itself than he had been when the enterprises would have fallen beneath his own control, and would have brought popularity to his own administration. He suggested an absurd way of preserving the sanctity of his doctrine in the abstract, while it was being shattered to fragments in practice. He drew up for the Virginia Legislature a verbose "Declaration and Protest," reciting the powerlessness of Congress in the premises, and closing with an enactment in general terms, whereby the State ratified and indorsed, by virtue of its own supreme power and authority in such matters, all the acts for internal improvements which Congress should pass in the future. This was silly, but Jefferson was greatly perturbed by what he saw going forward. He deemed the building of canals and roads with the national money a breach of the national compact such as might in time even justify a dissolution. For this, he said, the provocation was not yet sufficient; it was "the last resource, not to be thought of until much longer and greater sufferings;" but it was a possibility in the days to come. His alarm was groundless, and his cure useless. But Jefferson was growing old. This is the last of his interferences in public affairs which is worthy of mention.

CHAPTER XIX

AT MONTICELLO: PERSONAL MATTERS—DEATH

THERE WAS A strong theatrical tinge in Jefferson's composition. When he retired from the presidency it was to pose during his old age as the "Sage of Monticello," the good and wise old man, the benefactor of his kind, the statesman-philosopher. He recognized that it was proper, nay, incumbent, and even inevitable, to assume this role; he did it readily, without anxiety as to his perfect success in the part, and it must be acknowledged that he played it to the end very well. He at first expected to be the "hermit of Monticello;" but he soon found that he was of that class of hermits whose fame is so great among the nations that all the world flocks to gaze at them, so that retreat becomes a series of popular levees. The door of his mansion, hospitable even beyond Virginian precedent, stood ever open, and the stream of visitors passed ceaselessly in and out. Relatives came and brought their families, fathers and mothers with broods of children, and stayed for months; friends treated the generous roof-tree as their own; people of distinction or good social position claimed and received briefer entertainment. All this was pleasant, and the gratification given by such visitors generally more than offset the inconveniences. But it was less agreeable to have the imperfectly civilized people at large behave as if Monticello were the public domain where the ex-President was kept always on exhibition. Every one in the United States, of any enterprise, sooner or later found his way to this extraordinary "hermitage." The following amusing sketch of the household occurs in a letter quoted in Randall's Life: —

> We had persons from abroad, from all the States of the Union, from every part of the State, men, women, and children. In short, almost every day for at least eight months of the year brought its contingent of guests. People of wealth, fashion, men in office, professional men, military and civil, lawyers, doctors, Protestant clergymen, Catholic priests, members of Congress, foreign ministers, missionaries, Indian agents, tourists, travellers, artists, strangers, friends. Some came from affection and respect, some from curiosity, some to give or receive advice or instruction, some from idleness, some because others set the example.

The crowds actually invaded the house itself, and stood in the corridors to watch Jefferson pass from one room to another; they swarmed over the grounds and gaped at him as he walked beneath his trees or sat on his piazza. All this was flattering, but it was also extremely irksome; it too closely resembled the existence of the beast in the menagerie. Yet though Jefferson sometimes fled from it for a few days of hiding at a distant farm, he appears wonderfully seldom to have been lacking in the patient benignity which his part imposed upon him. The most impertinent had their gaze out unmolested; only a few complaints were made privately to friends.

In time that came to pass which Jefferson ought to have foreseen in the early stages of this fashion of life. He was keeping a large and naturally a very popular hotel, at which no guest ever thought of paying his score. The housekeeper at times had to provide fifty beds; inevitably the detail of slaves for the house and stables left few field hands for productive labor; all the produce of the Monticello estate was eaten up by the guests; and of course much other food and drink had to be purchased, and much wear and tear

to be made good. The form of entertainment was necessarily simple; yet Jefferson lived in what was deemed good style in that time
and neighborhood. Inevitably beneath these reducing processes
his fortune steadily and much too rapidly shrank. He had also experienced some severe blows. For example, the pre-revolutionary
debt upon his wife's estate was due in England, and the story of its
payment was very hard, though very honorable to him. In order to
meet it he sold some of her lands at a gold valuation, but finally got
the money in paper "worth two and a half per cent. of its nominal
value." This sum he deposited in the state treasury under a statute,
made during the Revolution, whereby debts owing to English subjects could be paid to the State, which then assumed the indebtedness and acquitted the debtor. But after the close of the war he
declined to avail himself of this acquittance.

"I am desirous of arranging with you," he wrote to the creditors, "such just and practicable conditions as will ascertain to you
the terms at which you will receive my part of your debt, and give
me the satisfaction of knowing that you are contented. What the
laws of Virginia are or may be, will in no wise influence my conduct. Substantial justice is my object, as decided by reason and not
by authority or compulsion. . . . I am ready to remove all difficulty
arising from this deposit, to take back to myself the demand against
the State, and to consider the deposit as originally made for myself
and not for you."

Thus the discharge of £3,749 12s. ultimately "swept nearly half
of his estate," while he got back from the state treasury so little that
he was wont to say concerning the land which he had parted with,
that he had "sold it for a great coat." This costly honesty appears
the more creditable, because Jefferson's financial resources had
been much diminished by the ravages of the British troops, of
which the money value, says Mr. Randall, "more than equalled the
amount of his British debt and its interest during the war."

Subsequently during his public life Jefferson sometimes lived

on his salary, sometimes exceeded it, and only while he was
Vice-President saved anything from it. Mr. Randall estimates his
property at $200,000 when he left the presidency, but, does not
make it perfectly clear whether or not this ought to be reduced by
the deduction of some indebtedness. It was a handsome amount;
but a part of it consisted of his house and furniture, and a very
expensive library; the remainder was lands and slaves, from which,
after the Monticello estate and negroes had been substantially neu-
tralized, as has been above explained, the net income was far from
equal to the demands upon it. Times and crops also often went
against him. When the owner of property thus invested once
begins to overrun his income, he enters on the road to ruin. By
degrees Jefferson became a poor man, and indeed worse than poor,
since he was involved in pecuniary embarrassments. Before matters had reached this stage he had sold his library to Congress for
$23,950; but this restorative did not long check the decline. In 1819
an indorsement which he had made for his friend, Wilson Cary
Nicholas, cost him $20,000. This blow consummated his ruin.
Nicholas is said to have been not blameworthy in the matter, but
the victim of ill fortune; and to have been crushed at the disaster
which he brought upon his friend. The kindness and delicacy with
which Jefferson took especial pains to treat him were remarkable,
and on one or two occasions were actually touching.

But debts must be paid, no matter how honored, good, or distinguished is the debtor, and ex-President Jefferson occupied no
better position than any other planter who was very near insolvency. It was an unfavorable time for turning a large estate into
money; and a sale in ordinary fashion would leave Jefferson substantially a pauper, even if not still a debtor. To avoid this he
desired to resort to a device then scarcely obsolete in Virginia. He
petitioned the Legislature for leave to dispose of his property at a
fair valuation by lottery. By this means, he said, "I can save the
house of Monticello, and a farm adjoining, to end my days in and

bury my bones. If not, I must sell house and all here and carry my family to Bedford, where I have not even a log hut to put my head into." When the proposition was broached some opposition was threatened, and its success was not certain. Jefferson wrote, with evident humiliation, "I perceive there are greater doubts than I had apprehended, whether the Legislature will indulge my request to them. It is a part of my mortification to perceive that I had so far overvalued myself as to have counted on it with too much confidence. I see," he sadly adds, "in the failure of this hope, a deadly blast of all my peace of mind during my remaining days." But he was spared a disappointment so severe. The opposition was feeble and the authorizing bill passed both houses by very gratifying majorities. The scheme, however, was not carried out. When the news of it spread through the country many offers of money were made. Public meetings were called, and subscriptions were started in the large cities. It seemed as though the people who, as Randall justly remarks, had literally eaten up most of the ex-President's property, would now restore it to him. Jefferson had repudiated the idea of a loan or gift from the state treasury, saying: "In any case I wish nothing from the treasury. The pecuniary compensations I have received for my services from time to time have been fully to my own satisfaction." But these offers of voluntary assistance from the people he was gratefully willing to accept. "I have spent three times as much money, and given my whole life to my countrymen," he said, "and now they nobly come forward in the only way they can; to repay me and save an old servant from being turned like a dog out of doors." "No cent of this is wrung from the tax-payer; it is the pure and unsolicited offering of love."

But though this liberality smoothed Jefferson's last days, it had little other effect; for before it had reached that stage at which it could complete his relief, he died. The debts still hung over his estate; the subscriptions of course ceased; the lottery proved a failure, and the executor had to dispose of all the assets. The lands brought ridiculously low prices,—three to ten dollars per acre,—and the proceeds did not pay the debts. But the executor himself made good the deficit, so that no creditor suffered through Jefferson's misfortunes.

The chief interest and occupation of Jefferson's last years were concentrated in establishing the University of Virginia, of which he was made Rector. In this business he labored with assiduity and success. But he encountered many obstacles and had some unworthy mortifications. He was especially vexed at the story which got abroad, and which impeded his efforts not a little, that he designed to give the college an anti-Christian character. It is needless to say that he had no such purpose; though he certainly did not intend it to be in the control of any especial creed. Jefferson's religious opinions, both during his life-time and since his death, have given rise to much controversy. His opponents constantly charged him with infidelity, his friends as vigorously denied the charge. The discussion annoyed and irritated him; but he would not put an end to it by making any statement concerning his belief. It was his private affair, he said with some temper, and he would not aid in establishing an inquisition of conscience. His grandson says that even his own family knew no more than the rest of the world concerning his religious opinions. One cannot but think that, had he been a firm believer in Christianity, he would probably not have regarded such reticence as justifiable, but would have felt it his duty to give to the faith the weight of his influence, which he well knew to be considerable. Nearly all the evidence which has been collected falls into the same scale, going to show that he was not a Christian in any strict sense of that word. It is true that the phrase bears widely different meanings to different persons; but probably the most liberal admissible interpretations would hardly make it apply to Jefferson. Mr. Randall says that he was a Christian, but founds the statement on evidence which goes to show only that Jefferson believed in a God or Supreme Being who concerned himself about the affairs of men. Of course this is by no means proof, perhaps not properly even evidence, of a belief in Christ. He went to church with tolerable regularity; he spoke with the utmost reverence of Christ as a moral teacher; but he carefully refrained from speaking of him as anything else than a human teacher. In the most interesting letter which he ever wrote on the subject, he says: "I am a Christian in the only sense in which he [Jesus] wished any one to be; sincerely attached to his doctrines in preference to all others; ascribing to himself every *human* excellence; and believing he never claimed any other." He compares Christ with Socrates and Epictetus, and says that when he died at about thirty-three years of age, his reason had "not yet attained the maximum of its energy, nor the course of his preaching, which was but of three years at most, presented occasions for developing a complete system of morals. Hence the doctrines which he really delivered were defective as a whole; and fragments only of what he did deliver have come to us, mutilated, misstated, and often untelligible." This hardly describes the Christian notion of God's revelation. After such language it was not worth while to add the saving clause, that "the question of his being a member of the Godhead, or in direct communication with it, . . . is foreign to the present view." To my mind it is very clear that Jefferson never believed that Christ was other than a human moralist, having no peculiar inspiration or divine connection, and differing from other moralists only as Shakespeare differs from other dramatists, namely, as greatly their superior in ability and fitness for his function. But those admirers of Jefferson, who themselves believe in the divinity of Christ, will probably refuse to accept this view, though they find themselves without sufficient evidence conclusively to confute it.

Jefferson, in his later years, became much concerned about the proper historical presentation of his times, and of the part played by himself and his party therein. He was probably the greatest letter writer who ever lived; he always wrote freely, and expressed himself vigorously. The latter part of his life was made a burden by his rule to give a full and sufficient answer to every civil letter which he received. Inevitably he sometimes fell into inconsistencies and errors; and sometimes said things which he would afterward wish unsaid. At times the thought of all that he had committed to paper alarmed him, and he declared that "the treacherous practice some people have of publishing one's letters, without leave" should be made "a penitentiary felony." Yet generally he regarded his own letters, "all preserved," written between 1790 and the close of his public life, as a great reservoir from which correct information could be drawn by posterity. He spoke with extreme acrimony of Marshall's "Life of Washington," as a purely partisan production. He was very much disturbed at the prospect of J. Q. Adams editing the writings of John Adams. "Doubtless," he said, "other things are in preparation, unknown to us. On our part we are depending on truth to make itself known, while history is taking a contrary set which may become too inveterate for correction." Shortly before his death he wrote to Madison: "To myself you have been a pillar of support through life. Take care of me when dead." All this anxiety lest the posthumous historical literature of the Federalists should have an influence with posterity superior to that of the Democrats; comes rather queerly from one who had the "Anas" secretly locked up in his desk. Yet his fears were justified by the event; the Federalists have to this day been more successful than the Republicans in getting their side forcibly and plausibly before the reading public.

The weaknesses of old age crept over Jefferson very gradually, as they are wont to do over sound and vigorous men. He had great dread of a helpless, and especially of an imbecile, senility, and watched for signs of mental decay with an almost morbid apprehensiveness. Certainly he suspected more symptoms of this evil than really existed; for though inevitably the vigor of his intellect became impaired in his extreme years; yet the clearness of his mind remained, even until the weakness of the closing hours began to deprive him of all knowledge of things earthly. There is very little complaining, at least in the published letters written in his last years; but there is a certain air of sombreness and melancholy. He could not well find fault with the career which had been allotted to him; but he could hardly recognize cheerfully that his usefulness was over, his authority a thing of the past, himself, while still alive, almost a character of history. His power had been too great to be cheerfully laid down. He appears to have been resigned, courageous, tranquil, and yet one gets the idea that as he drifted away from active affairs he was not happy, and that death must have lost its terrors for him some time before it actually came. The winter of 1826 found him evidently fast breaking. In the middle of March he made his will. In the spring we hear of him reading in the Bible, and the Greek tragedies; but he was not much longer able to do even this. As the 4th of July, 1826, approached he was known by himself, and by all the affectionate family-circle gathered around him, to be dying. He expressed a strong desire to live until that day should dawn; yet he seemed so weak, and the last laggard hours moved so slowly that his friends, to whom this wish of his seemed to have such a sanctity that they could not bear to have him disappointed, even in the almost unconscious hour of departure, feared that he would not endure so long. But life ebbed slowly from that strong frame. It was nearly one o'clock on that great day when he expired. John Adams was dead at Quincy a few hours earlier, with the words, "Thomas Jefferson still survives," struggling from his lips at the moment before they became silent forever. The triple coincidence is more singular than anything else of the kind in history.

APPENDIX

Judge Pickering. It seems that the language of the text concerning Judge Pickering does an unintentional injustice to the memory of a worthy man. Prof. Andrew P. Peabody, D. D., who is familiar with the local reminiscences and traditions concerning the judge, informs me that he was a man of excellent character and in the best repute in New Hampshire, and that the eccentricities and improprieties which served as the basis of his impeachment were only the earlier manifestations of a mental aberration which soon afterward developed into unquestionable insanity. Further authorities in favor of the judge may be found in William Plumer's *Life of William Plumer,* edited by Rev. Andrew P. Peabody, Boston, 1857, pp. 272–274; and in Nathaniel Adams' *Annals of Portsmouth,* Portsmouth, 1825, pp. 332–355.

INDEX

Adams, John, share in authorship of Declaration of Independence, 24; hostility to Washington, 25; unpopularity of, 25; share in debate on Declaration, 27; finds fault with Declaration, 27–28; charged by Jefferson with being a monarchist, 89; misunderstanding with Jefferson, growing out of publication of "Rights of Man," 92; elected President, 121–122; relations with Jefferson at time of his inauguration, 123–125; anger against France, 125; but sends new mission, in hopes of peace, 126; announces failure of French mission, 131; behavior concrning the X Y Z correspondence, 131; sends new mission to France, and divides Federalist party, 133–134;

defeated in election of 1800, 138; his "midnight appointments," 145; his retreat from Washington, 145; nominations of judges, 152–153; reconciliation with Jefferson, 225; death, 237

Adams, John Q., writes letters of Publicola, 92; goes over to the administrationists at time of the Embargo Bill, 208

Alien Act, passage of, 134

Ambuscade, captures the Grange, 105

"Anas," written by Jefferson, 77, 80; quoted, 82, 85, 87–89

Bishop, Samuel, appointment of, 154

Bonaparte, Napoleon, schemes for colonization in America, 168; issues decrees of Berlin and Milan, 205; remarks about the embargo, 215